SERIES

(ex•ploring)

1. Investigating in a systematic way: examining. 2. Searching into or ranging over for the purpose of discovery.

Getting Started with

Microsoft® OneNote® 2013

Mary Anne Poatsy

Linda Pogue

Series Created by Dr. Robert T. Grauer

PEARSON

Boston Columbus Indianapolis New York San Francisco Hoboken
Amsterdam Cape Town Dubai London Madrid Milan Munich Paris Montréal Toronto
Delhi Mexico City São Paulo Sydney Hong Kong Seoul Singapore Taipei Tokyo

Vice President of Career Skills: Andrew Gilfillan
Senior Editor: Samantha McAfee Lewis
Team Lead, Project Management: Laura Burgess
Project Manager: Laura Karahalis
Program Manager: Natacha Moore
Development Editor: Lori Damanti
Editorial Assistant: Victoria Lasavath
Director of Product Marketing: Maggie Waples
Director of Field Marketing: Leigh Ann Sims
Product Marketing Manager: Kaylee Carlson
Field Marketing Managers: Brad Forrester & Joanna Sabella
Marketing Coordinator: Susan Osterlitz
Senior Operations Specialist: Maura Zaldivar
Senior Art Director: Diane Ernsberger
Interior and Cover Design: Diane Ernsberger
Cover Photo: Courtesy of Shutterstock® Images
Associate Director of Design: Blair Brown
Digital Media Editor: Eric Hakanson
Director of Media Development: Taylor Ragan
Media Project Manager, Production: John Cassar
Full-Service Project Management: Jenna Vittorioso, Lumina Datamatics, Inc.
Composition: Lumina Datamatics, Inc.

Credits and acknowledgments borrowed from other sources and reproduced, with permission, in this textbook appear on the appropriate page within text.

Library of Congress Control Number: 2014940650

10 9 8 7 6 5 4 3 2

PEARSON

ISBN-10: 0-13-343432-X
ISBN-13: 978-0-13-343432-3

Dedications

To my husband, Charles, for his unwavering support in all my efforts, to my children, Susan and Scott, and their families. Thank you all for believing in me.

Linda Pogue

For my husband Ted, who unselfishly continues to take on more than his share to support me throughout the process; and for my children, Laura, Carolyn, and Teddy, whose encouragement and love have been inspiring.

Mary Anne Poatsy

About the Authors

Linda Pogue

Linda Pogue graduated magna cum laude from the University of Arkansas at Monticello in 2001 with a B.S. in Computer Information Systems and was awarded Information Systems Division Outstanding Senior of 2001. She earned an M.S. in Computer Information Systems from the University of Phoenix in 2003 and an M.S. in Education with an emphasis in Instructional Design for Online Learning from Capella University in 2009. After working as a programmer, she moved into the field of education. She has taught computer information courses at her alma mater—University of Arkansas at Monticello, Northwest Arkansas Community College, and Bryan College. After seven years of teaching, in 2011, she decided to go full time into authoring and technical editing of college-level supplements and textbooks.

Mary Anne Poatsy, Series Editor

Mary Anne is a senior faculty member at Montgomery County Community College, teaching various computer applications and concepts courses in face-to-face and online environments. She holds a B.A. in psychology and education from Mount Holyoke College and an M.B.A. in finance from Northwestern University's Kellogg Graduate School of Management.

Mary Anne has more than 12 years of educational experience. She is currently adjunct faculty at Gwynedd-Mercy College and Montgomery County Community College. She has also taught at Bucks County Community College and Muhlenberg College, as well as conducted personal training. Before teaching, she was Vice President at Shearson Lehman in the Municipal Bond Investment Banking Department.

Dr. Robert T. Grauer, Creator of the Exploring Series

Bob Grauer is an Associate Professor in the Department of Computer Information Systems at the University of Miami, where he is a multiple winner of the Outstanding Teaching Award in the School of Business, most recently in 2009. He has written numerous COBOL texts and is the vision behind the Exploring Office series, with more than three million books in print. His work has been translated into three foreign languages and is used in all aspects of higher education at both national and international levels. Bob Grauer has consulted for several major corporations including IBM and American Express. He received his Ph.D. in Operations Research in 1972 from the Polytechnic Institute of Brooklyn.

Contents

Microsoft OneNote 2013

Acknowledgments

The Exploring team would like to acknowledge and thank all the reviewers who helped us throughout the years by providing us with their invaluable comments, suggestions, and constructive criticism.

We'd like to especially thank our Focus Group attendees and User Diary Reviewers for this edition:

Stephen Z. Jourdan
Auburn University at Montgomery

Ann Rovetto
Horry-Georgetown Technical College

Jacqueline D. Lawson
Henry Ford Community College

Diane L. Smith
Henry Ford Community College

Sven Aelterman
Troy University

Suzanne M. Jeska
County College of Morris

Susan N. Dozier
Tidewater Community College

Robert G. Phipps Jr.
West Virginia University

Mike Michaelson
Palomar College

Mary Beth Tarver
Northwestern State University

Alexandre C. Probst
Colorado Christian University

Phil Nielson
Salt Lake Community College

Carolyn Barren
Macomb Community College

Sue A. McCrory
Missouri State University

Lucy Parakhovnik
California State University, Northridge

Jakie Brown Jr.
Stevenson University

Craig J. Peterson
American InterContinental University

Terry Ray Rigsby
Hill College

Biswadip Ghosh
Metropolitan State University of Denver

Cheryl Sypniewski
Macomb Community College

Lynn Keane
University of South Carolina

Sheila Gionfriddo
Luzerne College

Dick Hewer
Ferris State College

Carolyn Borne
Louisiana State University

Sumathy Chandrashekar
Salisbury University

Laura Marcoulides
Fullerton College

Don Riggs
SUNY Schenectady County Community College

Gary McFall
Purdue University

James Powers
University of Southern Indiana

James Brown
Central Washington University

Brian Powell
West Virginia University

Sherry Lenhart
Terra Community College

Chen Zhang
Bryant University

Nikia Robinson
Indian River State University

Jill Young
Southeast Missouri State University

Debra Hoffman
Southeast Missouri State University

Tommy Lu
Delaware Technical Community College

Mimi Spain
Southern Maine Community College

We'd like to thank everyone who has been involved in reviewing and providing their feedback, including for our previous editions:

Adriana Lumpkin
Midland College

Alan S. Abrahams
Virginia Tech

Ali Berrached
University of Houston–Downtown

Allen Alexander
Delaware Technical & Community College

Andrea Marchese
Maritime College, State University of New York

Andrew Blitz
Broward College; Edison State College

Angel Norman
University of Tennessee, Knoxville

Angela Clark
University of South Alabama

Ann Rovetto
Horry-Georgetown Technical College

Astrid Todd
Guilford Technical Community College

Audrey Gillant
Maritime College, State University of New York

Barbara Stover
Marion Technical College

Barbara Tollinger
Sinclair Community College

Ben Brahim Taha
Auburn University

Beverly Amer
Northern Arizona University

Beverly Fite
Amarillo College

Bonita Volker
Tidewater Community College

Bonnie Homan
San Francisco State University

Brad West
Sinclair Community College

Brian Powell
West Virginia University

Carol Buser
Owens Community College

Carol Roberts
University of Maine

Carolyn Barren
Macomb Community College

Cathy Poyner
Truman State University

Charles Hodgson
Delgado Community College

Cheri Higgins
Illinois State University

Cheryl Hinds
Norfolk State University

Chris Robinson
Northwest State Community College

Cindy Herbert
Metropolitan Community College–Longview

Dana Hooper
University of Alabama

Dana Johnson
North Dakota State University

Daniela Marghitu
Auburn University

David Noel
University of Central Oklahoma

David Pulis
Maritime College, State University of New York

David Thornton
Jacksonville State University

Dawn Medlin
Appalachian State University

Debby Keen
University of Kentucky

Debra Chapman
University of South Alabama

Derrick Huang
Florida Atlantic University

Diana Baran
Henry Ford Community College

Diane Cassidy
The University of North Carolina at Charlotte

Diane Smith
Henry Ford Community College

Don Danner
San Francisco State University

Don Hoggan
Solano College

Doncho Petkov
Eastern Connecticut State University

Donna Ehrhart
State University of New York at Brockport

Elaine Crable
Xavier University

Elizabeth Duett
Delgado Community College

Erhan Uskup
Houston Community College–Northwest

Eric Martin
University of Tennessee

Erika Nadas
Wilbur Wright College

Floyd Winters
Manatee Community College

Frank Lucente
Westmoreland County Community College

G. Jan Wilms
Union University

Gail Cope
Sinclair Community College

Gary DeLorenzo
California University of Pennsylvania

Gary Garrison
Belmont University

George Cassidy
Sussex County Community College

Gerald Braun
Xavier University

Gerald Burgess
Western New Mexico University

Gladys Swindler
Fort Hays State University

Heith Hennel
Valencia Community College

Henry Rudzinski
Central Connecticut State University

Irene Joos
La Roche College

Iwona Rusin
Baker College; Davenport University

J. Roberto Guzman
San Diego Mesa College

Jan Wilms
Union University

Jane Stam
Onondaga Community College

Janet Bringhurst
Utah State University

Jeanette Dix
Ivy Tech Community College

Jennifer Day
Sinclair Community College

Jill Canine
Ivy Tech Community College

Jim Chaffee
The University of Iowa Tippie College of Business

Joanne Lazirko
University of Wisconsin–Milwaukee

Jodi Milliner
Kansas State University

John Hollenbeck
Blue Ridge Community College

John Seydel
Arkansas State University

Judith A. Scheeren
Westmoreland County Community College

Judith Brown
The University of Memphis

Juliana Cypert
Tarrant County College

Kamaljeet Sanghera
George Mason University

Karen Priestly
Northern Virginia Community College

Karen Ravan
Spartanburg Community College

Kathleen Brenan
Ashland University

Ken Busbee
Houston Community College

Kent Foster
Winthrop University

Kevin Anderson
Solano Community College

Kim Wright
The University of Alabama

Kristen Hockman
University of Missouri–Columbia

Kristi Smith
Allegany College of Maryland

Laura McManamon
University of Dayton

Leanne Chun
Leeward Community College

Lee McClain
Western Washington University

Linda D. Collins
Mesa Community College

Linda Johnsonius
Murray State University

Linda Lau
Longwood University

Linda Theus
Jackson State Community College

Linda Williams
Marion Technical College

Lisa Miller
University of Central Oklahoma

Lister Horn
Pensacola Junior College

Lixin Tao
Pace University

Loraine Miller
Cayuga Community College

Lori Kielty
Central Florida Community College

Lorna Wells
Salt Lake Community College

Lorraine Sauchin
Duquesne University

Lucy Parakhovnik (Parker)
California State University, Northridge

Lynn Mancini
Delaware Technical Community College

Mackinzee Escamilla
South Plains College

Marcia Welch
Highline Community College

Margaret McManus
Northwest Florida State College

Margaret Warrick
Allan Hancock College

Marilyn Hibbert
Salt Lake Community College

Mark Choman
Luzerne County Community College

Mary Duncan
University of Missouri–St. Louis

Melissa Nemeth
Indiana University-Purdue University Indianapolis

Melody Alexander
Ball State University

Michael Douglas
University of Arkansas at Little Rock

Michael Dunklebarger
Alamance Community College

Michael G. Skaff
College of the Sequoias

Michele Budnovitch
Pennsylvania College of Technology

Mike Jochen
East Stroudsburg University

Mike Scroggins
Missouri State University

Muhammed Badamas
Morgan State University

NaLisa Brown
University of the Ozarks

Nancy Grant
Community College of Allegheny County–South Campus

Nanette Lareau
University of Arkansas Community College–Morrilton

Pam Brune
Chattanooga State Community College

Pam Uhlenkamp
Iowa Central Community College

Patrick Smith

Marshall Community and Technical College

Paul Addison
Ivy Tech Community College

Paula Ruby
Arkansas State University

Peggy Burrus
Red Rocks Community College

Peter Ross
SUNY Albany

Philip H. Nielson
Salt Lake Community College

Ralph Hooper
University of Alabama

Ranette Halverson
Midwestern State University

Richard Blamer
John Carroll University

Richard Cacace
Pensacola Junior College

Richard Hewer
Ferris State University

Rob Murray
Ivy Tech Community College

Robert Dušek
Northern Virginia Community College

Robert Sindt
Johnson County Community College

Robert Warren
Delgado Community College

Rocky Belcher
Sinclair Community College

Roger Pick
University of Missouri at Kansas City

Ronnie Creel
Troy University

Rosalie Westerberg
Clover Park Technical College

Ruth Neal
Navarro College

Sandra Thomas
Troy University

Sheila Gionfriddo
Luzerne County Community College

Sherrie Geitgey
Northwest State Community College

Sophia Wilberscheid
Indian River State College

Sophie Lee
California State University, Long Beach

Stacy Johnson
Iowa Central Community College

Stephanie Kramer
Northwest State Community College

Stephen Jourdan
Auburn University Montgomery

Steven Schwarz
Raritan Valley Community College

Sue McCrory
Missouri State University

Susan Fuschetto
Cerritos College

Susan Medlin
UNC Charlotte

Suzan Spitzberg
Oakton Community College

Sven Aelterman
Troy University

Sylvia Brown
Midland College

Tanya Patrick
Clackamas Community College

Terri Holly
Indian River State College

Thomas Rienzo
Western Michigan University

Tina Johnson
Midwestern State University

Tommy Lu
Delaware Technical and Community College

Troy S. Cash
Northwest Arkansas Community College

Vicki Robertson
Southwest Tennessee Community

Weifeng Chen
California University of Pennsylvania

Wes Anthony
Houston Community College

William Ayen
University of Colorado at Colorado Springs

Wilma Andrews
Virginia Commonwealth University

Yvonne Galusha
University of Iowa

Special thanks to our development and technical team:

Lori Damanti

Michael Gordon

Julie Boyles

Morgan Hetzler

Preface

The Exploring Series and You

Exploring is Pearson's Office Application series that requires students like you to think "beyond the point and click." In this edition, we have worked to restructure the Exploring experience around the way you, today's modern student, actually use your resources.

The goal of Exploring is, as it has always been, to go further than teaching just the steps to accomplish a task—the series provides the theoretical foundation for you to understand when and why to apply a skill.

As a result, you achieve a deeper understanding of each application and can apply this critical thinking beyond Office and the classroom.

You are practical students, focused on what you need to do to be successful in this course and beyond, and want to be as efficient as possible. Exploring has evolved to meet you where you are and help you achieve success efficiently. Pearson has paid attention to the habits of students today, how you get information, how you are motivated to do well in class, and what your future goals look like. We asked you and your peers for acceptance of new tools we designed to address these points, and you responded with a resounding "YES!"

Here Is What We Learned About You

You are goal-oriented. You want a good grade in this course—so we rethought how Exploring works so that you can learn the how and why behind the skills in this course to be successful now. You also want to be successful in your future career—so we used motivating case studies to show relevance of these skills to your future careers and incorporated Soft Skills, Collaboration, and Analysis Cases in this edition to set you up for success in the future.

You read, prepare, and study differently than students used to. You use textbooks like a tool—you want to easily identify what you need to know and learn it efficiently. We have added key features such as Step Icons, Hands-On Exercise Videos, and tracked everything via page numbers that allow you to navigate the content efficiently, making the concepts accessible and creating a map to success for you to follow.

You go to college now with a different set of skills than students did five years ago. The new edition of Exploring moves you beyond the basics of the software at a faster pace, without sacrificing coverage of the fundamental skills that you need to know. This ensures that you will be engaged from page 1 to the end of the book.

You and your peers have diverse learning styles. With this in mind, we broadened our definition of "student resources" to include Compass, an online skill database; movable Student Reference cards; Hands-On Exercise videos to provide a secondary lecture-like option of review; Soft Skills video exercises to illustrate important non-technical skills; and the most powerful online homework and assessment tool around with a direct 1:1 content match with the Exploring Series, MyITLab. Exploring will be accessible to all students, regardless of learning style.

Providing You with a Map to Success to Move Beyond the Point and Click

All of these changes and additions will provide you with an easy and efficient path to follow to be successful in this course, regardless of your learning style or any existing knowledge you have at the outset. Our goal is to keep you more engaged in both the hands-on and conceptual sides, helping you to achieve a higher level of understanding that will guarantee you success in this course and in your future career. In addition to the vision and experience of the series creator, Robert T. Grauer, we have assembled a tremendously talented team of Office Applications authors who have devoted themselves to teaching you the ins and outs of Microsoft Word, Excel, Access, and PowerPoint. Led in this edition by series editor Mary Anne Poatsy, the whole team is equally dedicated to providing you with a **map to success** to support the Exploring mission of **moving you beyond the point and click**.

Key Features

- **White Pages/Yellow Pages** clearly distinguish the theory (white pages) from the skills covered in the Hands-On Exercises (yellow pages) so students always know what they are supposed to be doing.
- **Enhanced Objective Mapping** enables students to follow a directed path through each chapter, from the objectives list at the chapter opener through the exercises in the end of chapter.
    - **Objectives List:** This provides a simple list of key objectives covered in the chapter. This includes page numbers so students can skip between objectives where they feel they need the most help.
    - **Step Icons:** These icons appear in the white pages and reference the step numbers in the Hands-On Exercises, providing a correlation between the two so students can easily find conceptual help when they are working hands-on and need a refresher.
    - **Quick Concepts Check:** A series of questions that appear briefly at the end of each white page section. These questions cover the most essential concepts in the white pages required for students to be successful in working the Hands-On Exercises. Page numbers are included for easy reference to help students locate the answers.
    - **Chapter Objectives Review:** Appears toward the end of the chapter and reviews all important concepts throughout the chapter. Newly designed in an easy-to-read bulleted format.
- **Key Terms Matching:** A new exercise that requires students to match key terms to their definitions. This requires students to work actively with this important vocabulary and prove conceptual understanding.
- **Case Study** presents a scenario for the chapter, creating a story that ties the Hands-On Exercises together.
- **End-of-Chapter Exercises** offer instructors several options for assessment. Each chapter has approximately 12–15 exercises ranging from multiple choice questions to open-ended projects. Newly included in this is a Key Terms Matching exercise of approximately 20 questions, as well as a Collaboration Case and Soft Skills Case for every chapter.

ANALYSIS CASE

CREATIVE CASE

- **Enhanced Mid-Level Exercises** include a **Creative Case** (for PowerPoint and Word), which allows students some flexibility and creativity, not being bound by a definitive solution, and an **Analysis Case** (for Excel and Access), which requires students to interpret the data they are using to answer an analytic question, as well as **Discover Steps**, which encourage students to use Help or to problem-solve to accomplish a task.

Instructor Resources

The Instructor's Resource Center, available at www.pearsonhighered.com, includes the following:

- **Instructor Manual** provides an overview of all available resources as well as student data and solution files for every exercise.
- **Solution Files with Scorecards** assist with grading the Hands-On Exercises and end-of-chapter exercises.
- **Prepared Exams** allow instructors to assess all skills covered in a chapter with a single project.
- **Rubrics** for Mid-Level Creative Cases and Beyond the Classroom Cases in Microsoft Word format enable instructors to customize the assignments for their classes.
- **PowerPoint Presentations** with notes for each chapter are included for out-of-class study or review.
- **Objectives Lists** map chapter objectives to Hands-On Exercises and end-of-chapter exercises.
- **Multiple Choice, Key Term Matching, and Quick Concepts Check Answer Keys**
- **Test Bank** provides objective-based questions for every chapter.
- **Syllabus Templates**
- **Scripted Lectures** offer an in-class lecture guide for instructors to mirror the Hands-on-Exercises.

Student Resources

Companion Web Site

www.pearsonhighered.com/exploring offers expanded IT resources and self-student tools for students to use for each chapter, including:

- Online Chapter Review
- Glossary
- Chapter Objectives Review

OneNote 2013

CHAPTER 1

Getting Started with OneNote 2013

Create, Manage, Integrate, and Synchronize OneNote Notebooks

berc/fotolia

OBJECTIVES AFTER YOU READ THIS CHAPTER, YOU WILL BE ABLE TO:

1. Create and Manage Notebooks p. 2
2. Add Content to OneNote 2013 p. 18
3. Integrate Office Files p. 26

CASE STUDY | Pearson University Majors

Bonnie Duckett is an undergraduate student majoring in Information Systems Management in the College of Technology & Computing at Pearson University, a prestigious university on the East Coast. Last semester, Bonnie lost an important spiral notebook containing study notes for her Basic Programming class, which caused issues when it was time to study for final exams.

This semester her Systems Analysis and Design Methods instructor, Dr. Vamil Singh, has recommended that she use OneNote to track course and lecture notes, appointments, and assignments. Bonnie is excited about the various possibilities for taking and keeping track of her notes, and wants to learn more about the application.

Introduction to OneNote

Notes in one form or another are a part of our lives. Whether they are used to remind us of important dates, to pick up our dry cleaning, or how to complete a specific task on the computer, notes help keep us on track. With the invention of Post-it Notes, 3M's handy stick up notes, many of us now work in paper studded office areas and homes. Unfortunately, if the note you need at home is stuck to your work computer monitor, you do not have access to it without returning to work.

First introduced in 2003 for the Windows XP Tablet PC, the OneNote application makes note taking simple. OneNote is a note taking software used by students, office assistants, managers, and professionals to keep track of important information and tasks. With the advent of the Cloud, ***OneNote 2013***, Microsoft's digital note taking software, makes it possible to access your notes from home, school, office, or any location or computing device that has Internet access. OneNote 2013 works with desktop computers, laptops, tablets, and some smartphones. For the desktop version of OneNote 2013, computers must have Windows 7 or newer Windows operating systems. There are also versions of OneNote designed to work with non-Microsoft operating systems, such Apple's iOS and Google's Android.

FIGURE 1.1 OneNote is similar in concept to a spiral notebook with multiple tabbed sections.

Creating and Managing OneNote Notebooks

In this section, you will learn how to create and manage OneNote 2013 notebooks on your desktop or laptop computer. You will add sections and pages, rename and organize sections and pages, and print and export sections and pages. To better understand the concept behind OneNote 2013, think of the familiar spiral notebook with multiple tabbed ***sections***, as shown in Figure 1.1. Within each section, there are multiple pages. Unlike a spiral notebook with its fixed capacity, OneNote has an unlimited number of notebooks. Each ***notebook*** has an unlimited number of sections, and each section has an unlimited number of ***pages***. If a single notebook becomes large enough to be unwieldy, a new one can be created at any time. The instructions in this text are based on using OneNote in Windows 8.1.

To open OneNote in Windows 8.1, click the OneNote 2013 tile on the Start screen. If Microsoft Office has been installed on your system, but the OneNote 2013 tile is not available on the Start screen, click the Apps button at the bottom of the Start screen to locate the OneNote 2013 tile. Right-click the tile, and then at the bottom of the screen, click Pin to Start. When you start OneNote 2013 for the first time, the system will have to set up your application. If you have a Microsoft account and have signed into the account, after a short wait, OneNote will open with a Quick Notes section displaying. When the First things first window displays, read the text, and then select one of the options. For purposes of this text, you can select No thanks, if you wish. Before continuing, you must click Accept. If you wish to read the Microsoft Office License Agreement before accepting it, click View Agreement. If you do not have a Microsoft account, OneNote will open with a blank Section containing a blank page. Some features, such as syncing your notebook to OneDrive, formerly SkyDrive, will require you to create a Microsoft account. Syncing the notebook to OneDrive mirrors the notebook on the cloud, so that all Internet-connected devices can access the same content. A Microsoft account can be created through www.onedrive.com, www.live.com, or www.outlook.com.

TIP If You Do Not Have OneNote 2013

This book assumes you already have Microsoft OneNote 2013 installed on your computer. If not, you can purchase, download, and install the application from http://www.microsoftstore.com/ or download a free app through the Microsoft Store tile on your Windows 8.1 Start screen.

The first time you open OneNote, the application creates a new notebook named *default name Notebook* with *default name* being replaced by the user name on the computer. If the OneNote application has been previously opened, the notebook that was open when you closed the application will open. If no notebooks were open when the application was previously closed, you will see the message, "You do not have any open notebooks." In fresh install of OneNote, the Quick Notes section opens on the *OneNote: one place for all of your notes* page. This page has information about OneNote on the page.

Scroll down and read all the information available. On the right side of the screen, click the OneNote Basics page tab. The OneNote Basics page demonstrates some of what you can do with OneNote, including creating To-do lists, inserting screenshots of Web pages, inserting tables, adding annotations to charts, and much more. See Figure 1.2.

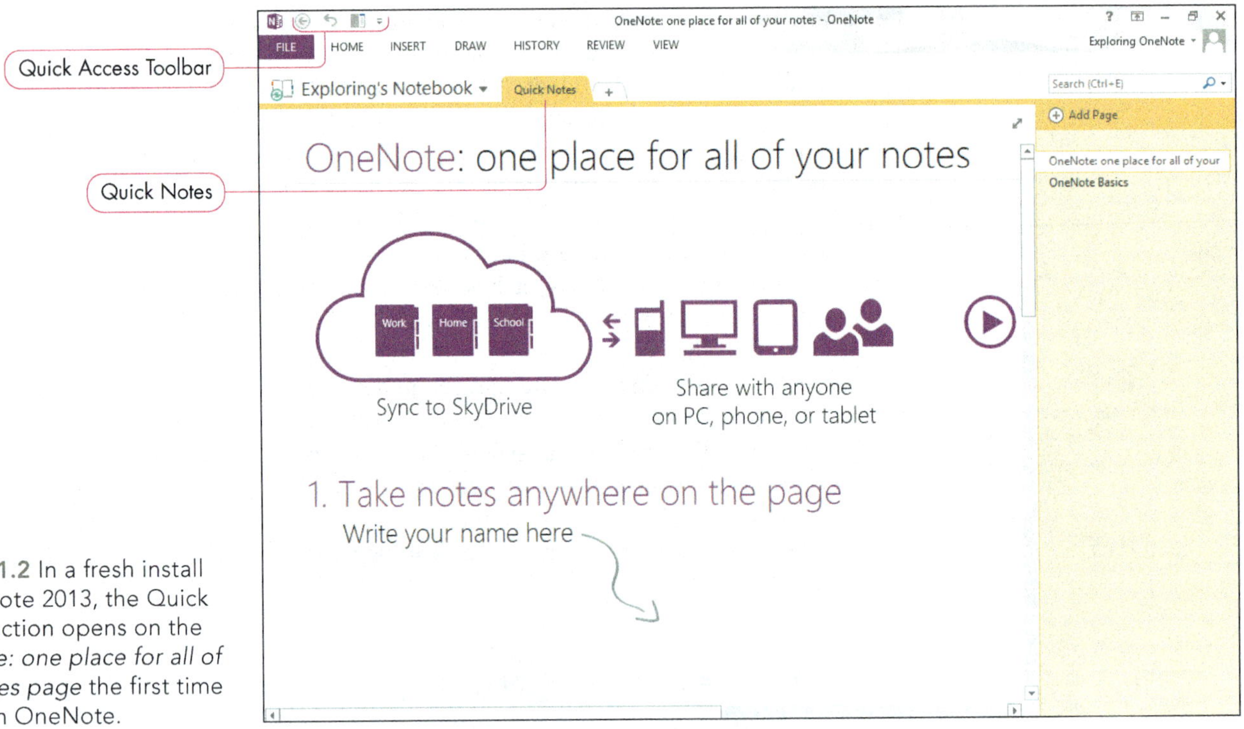

FIGURE 1.2 In a fresh install of OneNote 2013, the Quick Notes section opens on the *OneNote: one place for all of your notes page* the first time you open OneNote.

Discovering the OneNote 2013 Interface

At the top left corner of the window, the ***Quick Access Toolbar*** in OneNote contains four command buttons: Back, Undo, Dock to Desktop, and Customize Quick Access Toolbar. Similar to most Microsoft Office applications, the OneNote 2013 interface features a ***Ribbon*** that contains tabs. If the Ribbon does not display, right-click any menu item, such as VIEW, and then click Collapse the Ribbon. Each tab, FILE, HOME, INSERT, DRAW, HISTORY, REVIEW, and VIEW, contains groups of commands that enable you to manage, manipulate, and format your OneNote page contents. Contextual tabs are tabs that only display when you are working with specific items such as tables, equations, or audio or video recordings. For instance, when a table is inserted on a page, while the table is still selected, the contextual TABLE TOOLS LAYOUT tab displays. The Ribbon can be collapsed to give more room for the page area. To collapse the Ribbon, click the Collapse the Ribbon button above the right end of the Search box. The Notebook Pane only displays if you press the down arrow on the Notebook Pane tab, which is to the left of the Section tabs. From the ***Notebook Pane***, you can access other OneNote notebooks, add a notebook, or open notebooks not listed. ***Section tabs*** make it possible to keep content types separated. You might create a notebook for this semester's work titled Fall Semester. Inside that notebook you would add sections devoted to each class being taken this semester. Within each section, you might have a general notes page, an assignments page, and a research page. By having different sections, the specific content you need is easy to locate.

The ***Search bar*** consists of a text box, a magnifying glass search icon, and a Change *Search Scope* arrow that provides the option to change ***search scope*** parameters, which determine where OneNote searches to find key terms. Parameter choices are Find on This Page, This Section, This Section Group, This Notebook, and All Notebooks, with the option to set any of these as the default search scope. The ***Page Pane***, located on the right side of the screen, shows page tabs for all pages included in the current selected section. Subpage tabs are indented below the page tabs to which they are attached. The page area is the actual page to which you will add content. In the top right corner of the page area, there is a diagonal double pointed arrow. This is your Full Page View button. In Full Page view, the Ribbon and Section tabs are hidden. To return to Normal view, click the diagonal pointed arrow Normal View button. See Table 1.1.

TABLE 1.1 OneNote 2013 Interface

Quick Access Toolbar	By default, the Quick Access toolbar contains four command buttons: a Back button, an Undo button, a Dock to Desktop button, and a Customize Quick Access Toolbar button.
Ribbon	The Ribbon has seven tabs, FILE, HOME, INSERT, DRAW, HISTORY, REVIEW, and VIEW. The tabs provide easy access to commands for formatting and managing content in your pages.
Notebook Pane	By default, this is minimized. In its maximized position, the Notebook Pane lists notebooks, allowing you to easily switch between notebooks.
Section Tabs	The section tabs display the sections in your notebook, and provide an easy way to add a new section.
Search Bar	The Search bar allows you to search for content within your notebook.
Page Pane	The Page Pane displays tabs for pages located within the selected Section.
Page Area	The Page Area is the current page displayed in the center of your screen. This is where you will add content to your notebook.

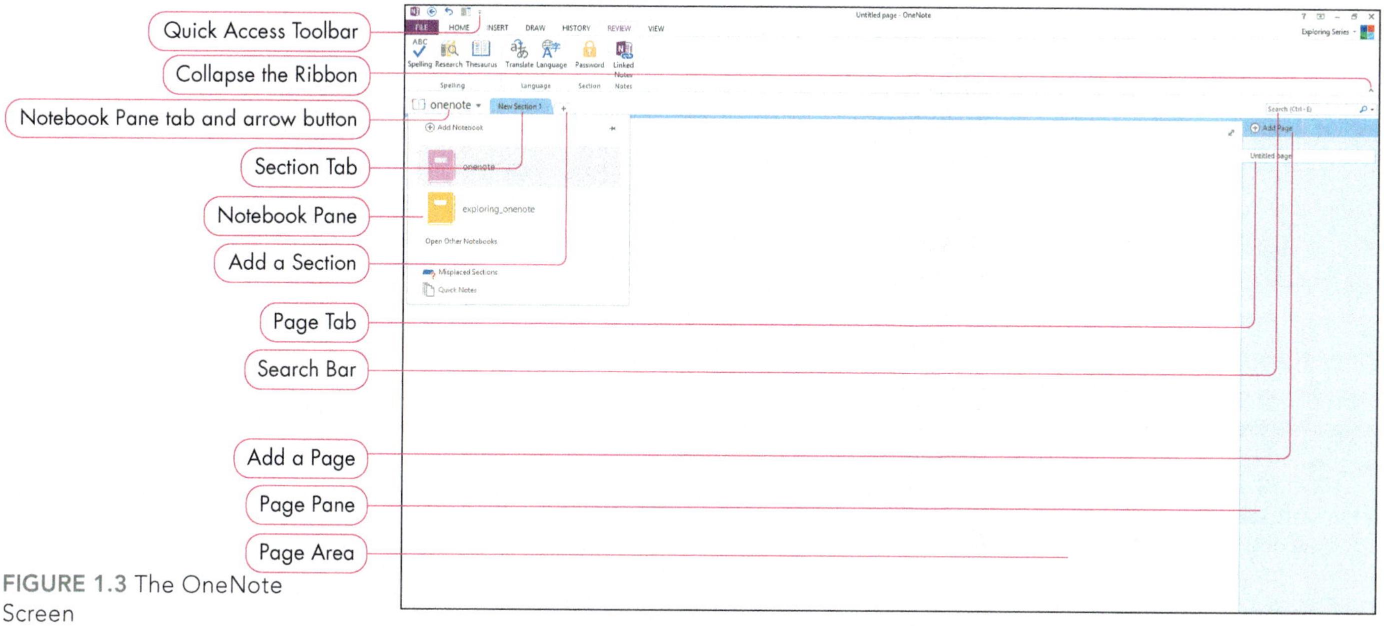

FIGURE 1.3 The OneNote Screen

Create a Notebook and Add Sections and Pages

STEP 1» Because OneNote allows you to create as many notebooks as you need, you can create separate notebooks for different areas of your life. You might create a different notebook for home and family, school, and work. Within each notebook, you can create appropriate sections. For your home and family notebook, you might have a section for family phone numbers and addresses, a section for birthdays, and another section to keep track of prescriptions. For the school notebook, you might have a section for each class with pages for lecture notes, homework, research, and schedules. For your work notebook, you might have a section for coworkers where you have pages for phone numbers, a section for project notes and target dates, and another for team activities. See Figure 1.4 for Backstage view.

To create a new notebook, follow these steps:

1. Open OneNote. If necessary, display the Ribbon.
2. Click FILE to open Backstage view, and then click New.
3. In the New Notebook window, navigate to the location where the notebook should be saved, such as your storage device or OneDrive.
4. Name the notebook.
5. Click Create Notebook.

When you create a new notebook, it opens with a default section titled New Section 1. The default section contains one Untitled page. To add a new section, select from one of the two following methods:

- Right-click on an existing Section tab, and then click New Section.
- Click the small tab with a (+) sign on it.

There are three ways to add a new page to a section:

- Right-click on an existing page tab, and then click New Page.
- Click the Add Page command at the top of the Page navigation pane.
- Press Ctrl+N.

To make a page into a subpage, right-click on the Page tab, and then click Make Subpage. A ***subpage*** is indented below the page to which it is attached.

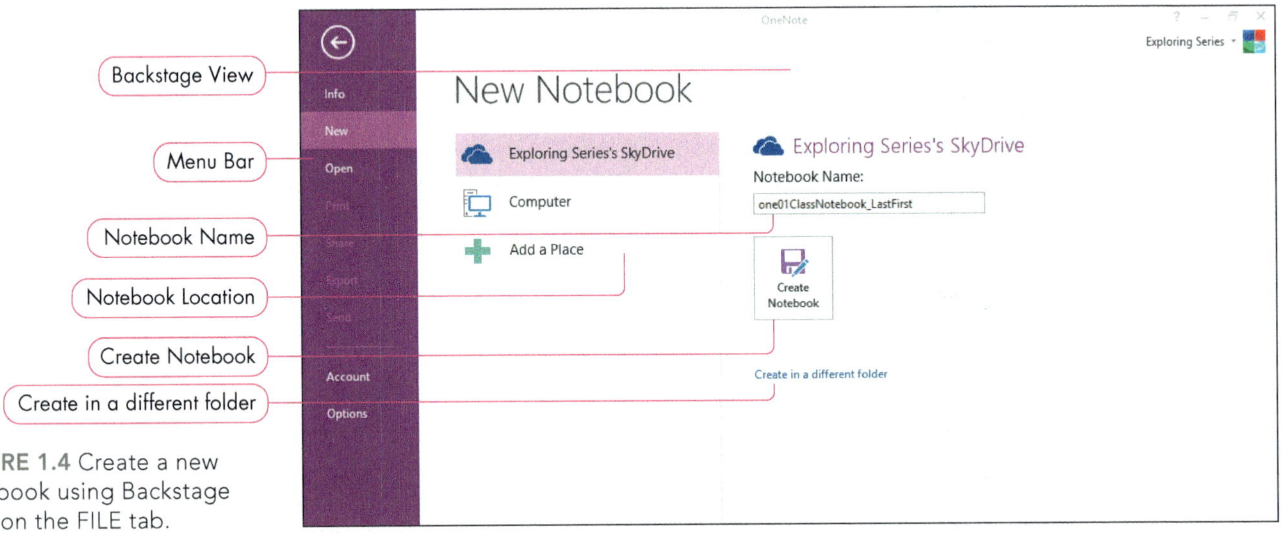

FIGURE 1.4 Create a new notebook using Backstage view on the FILE tab.

Delete and Rename Sections and Pages

STEP 2» With multiple ways to complete deleting and renaming sections and pages, you can select the method that works best for the way you work. There are three methods that can be used to delete a section or a page. First, select the Section or Page tab that should be deleted, then use one of the following methods:

- Right-click the section or page tab, and then click Delete.
- On the Home tab, in the Basic Text group, click Delete.
- Press the Delete key on the keyboard.

There are two methods to rename a section:

- Right-click the Section tab, and then click Rename. Type the new section name, and then press Enter.
- Double-click the section tab, type the new name, and then press Enter.

There are two ways to rename a page:

- In the Page pane, right-click the Page tab, and then click Rename. Type the page name and then press Enter.
- With the page displayed, highlight the page title, and then type the new page title.

If a section or page is accidentally deleted, you can retrieve the section or page until the Recycle Bin has been emptied. To retrieve a section or page you deleted, click the HISTORY tab, in the History group, click the upper half of the Notebook Recycle Bin, right-click the tab of the section or page you need to retrieve, and use the Move or Copy command to move the section or page back to the original notebook. If you do not find the section or page you want to retrieve, make sure you are in the notebook from which the section or page was deleted. Each notebook has its own separate Recycle Bin.

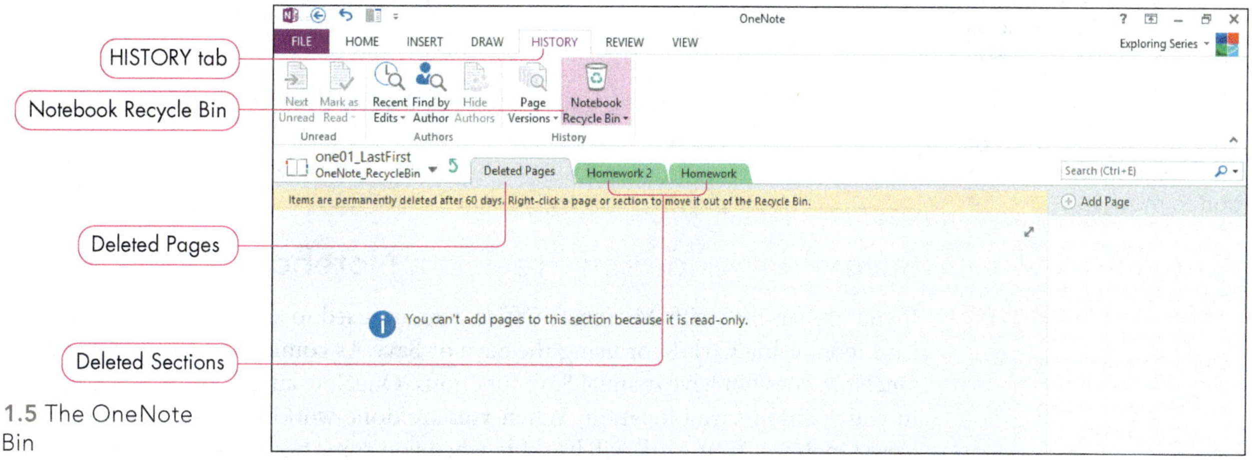

FIGURE 1.5 The OneNote Recycle Bin

Copy or Move a Notebook Section to Another Notebook

STEP 3» Occasionally, you may find you created a section in the wrong notebook, or you may need the same section in multiple notebooks. To copy an existing section to a new notebook:

1. Right-click on the section tab.
2. Click Move or Copy.
3. Select the notebook to which you wish to copy the section.
4. Click Copy.

You can use the same technique to move a section to an existing notebook, but instead of clicking Copy, click Move. If you copy a section to another notebook, the original section remains in the original notebook. If you move the section, the original notebook no longer contains the section. See Figure 1.6.

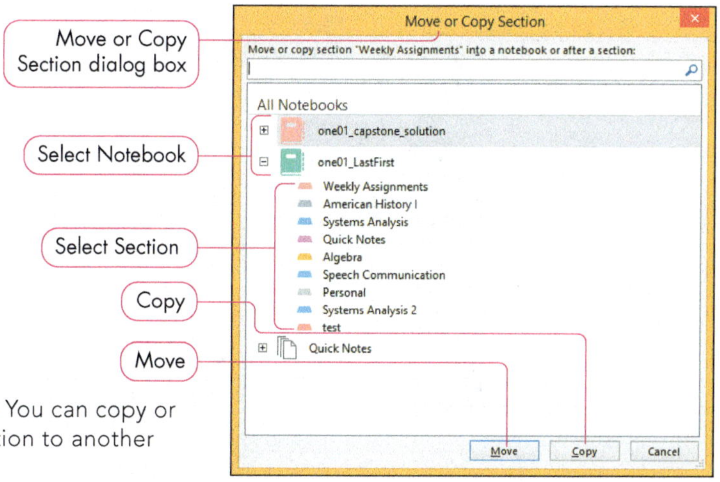

FIGURE 1.6 You can copy or move a section to another notebook.

Rearrange Sections and Pages, and Merge Sections

STEP 4

New sections are added to the right of existing section tabs. When a new section is added, it might be more logical to have that section as the first tab. To rearrange section tabs, make the tab you wish to move the active section, click the tab and drag the section tab to the desired location. Within sections, page tabs can be rearranged, too. Select the page tab you wish to move, left-click on the page tab, and hold down the mouse button while dragging the page tab to the new location. There may be times when it makes sense to combine two or more sections. To ***merge*** a section with another section, right-click the section you wish to merge, click Merge into Another Section, select the section you want the section to merge with, and then click Merge.

An arrow indicates where the section will move when the mouse button is released

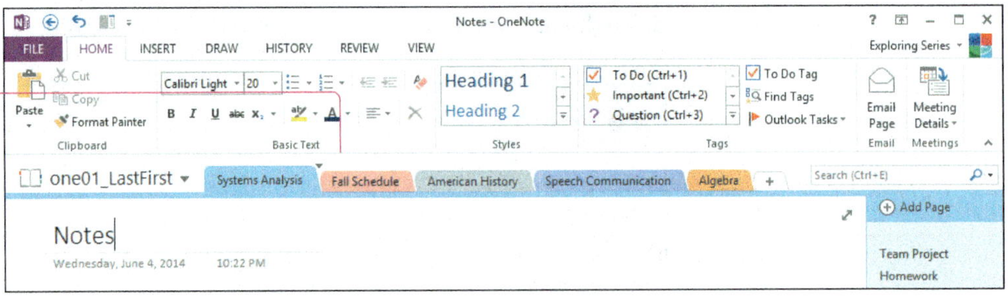

FIGURE 1.7 An arrow indicates the new location of a section when you drag a section to move it.

Save, Print, and Print Preview a Notebook

STEP 5

If you are familiar with Microsoft Office, you are used to saving your work by clicking the Save icon, using Ctrl+S, or using the Save or Save As commands on the File tab. However, OneNote does not have manual Save functions. OneNote automatically saves your notebook to your chosen saved location. When you are done working with your notebook, simply close OneNote. Your work will be there when you come back to the notebook.

There may be times you need to print your notebook. You may want to have your study notes in a more portable format. To print a notebook:

1. Click the FILE tab.
2. Click Print.
3. Click the Print button. The Print Dialog box will open.
4. Select the desired printer.
5. Click Print.

For more control over what is printed, after clicking the Print in Backstage view, click the Print Preview button. The Print Preview and Settings dialog box will open, giving you the options to select your print range, select your paper size and orientation, and add a footer and page numbers before printing. See Figure 1.8.

Print Preview and Settings dialog box

Print range

Paper size

Orientation

Footer

Start page numbering at 1

Print

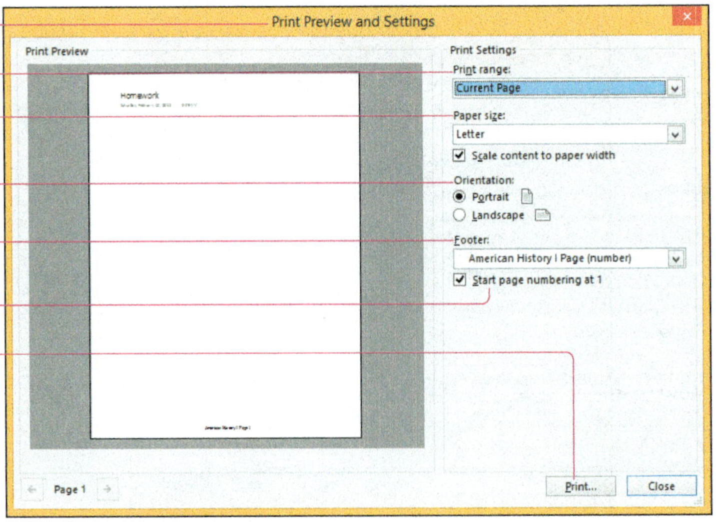

FIGURE 1.8 The Print Preview and Settings dialog box gives you the option to add a footer and page numbers before printing.

Send Notes using Outlook

To send notes through e-mail, you must have Outlook 2013 set up on your computer. To e-mail note pages:

1. On the HOME tab, in the Email group, click Email Page.
2. In the Outlook email message window, type the recipient in the To text box.
3. Type a subject line in the Subject text box.
4. Type your message in the Message text box.
5. Click the Send button.

Once your e-mail account is set up, an additional group, Meeting, will appear at the right end of the HOME tab. The Meeting Details command will enable you to review the details of appointments and meetings set up in your Outlook account. See Figure 1.9.

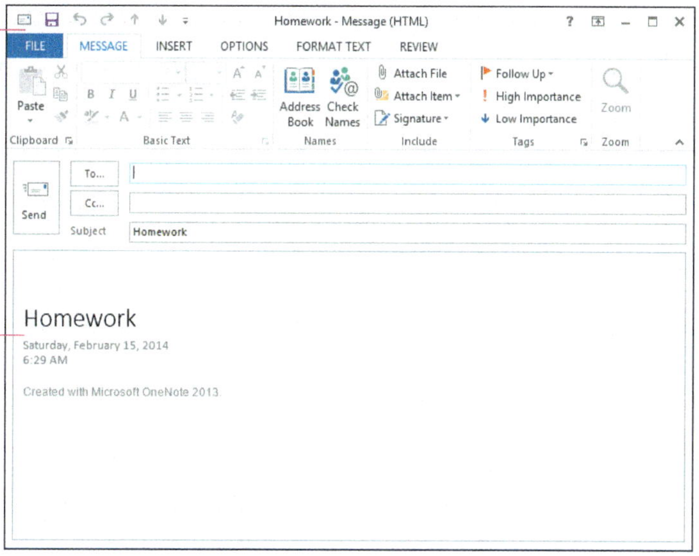

FIGURE 1.9 Using Outlook, you can send notes by e-mail to colleagues.

Export a Notebook

While storing a OneNote notebook on the cloud and sharing it with others is a good way to provide business essential information to team members and colleagues, there are times when you will need to save a backup of the notebook to a different storage media. Using the ***Export*** command on Backstage View on the FILE tab, you can save the entire notebook, a page, a group, or a section to a different location. Another reason to use Export would be to create a new notebook based on a previous notebook. To export an entire notebook:

1. Open the notebook to be exported.
2. Click the FILE tab.
3. Click Export.
4. Select Notebook in the Export Current section.
5. Select OneNote Package (*.onepkg) in the Select Format section.
6. Click Export.
7. Navigate to the correct storage device.
8. Change the file name if desired.
9. Click Save.

To restore a *.onepkg, in your File Explorer, navigate to the location to which the file was saved, and then double-click the file name. In the Unpack Notebook dialog box, verify the name of the notebook and the ***path*** to the notebook location, and then click Create. The path tells the computer which drive or library the folder holding the notebook will be created. The notebook will open in OneNote 2013 desktop application.

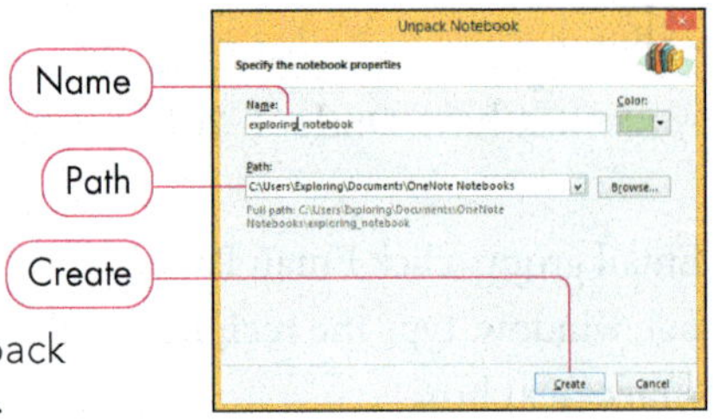

FIGURE 1.10 The Unpack Notebook dialog box.

Quick Concepts

1. What sections and pages would you create in a notebook for personal information? ***p. 5***
2. If a section is accidentally deleted, what steps would you take to retrieve it? ***p. 7***
3. Explain how printing works in OneNote. ***p. 8***
4. List two reasons you might need to export a notebook to a USB drive. ***p. 9***

Hands-On Exercises

1 Creating and Managing OneNote Notebooks

After providing a short introduction to OneNote, Dr. Singh recommended that Becky create a notebook to keep track of her school courses. You have offered to help Becky create her notebook and set it up to be useful.

Skills covered: Create a Notebook and Add Sections and Pages • Delete and Rename Sections and Pages • Copy a Section to Another Notebook • Rearrange Sections and Pages • Add a Footer, Print a Section, and Send a Section

STEP 1 » CREATE A NOTEBOOK AND ADD SECTIONS AND PAGES

After creating a notebook for course work, add course sections and pages to the notebook. Refer to Figures 1.11 and 1.12 as you complete Step 1.

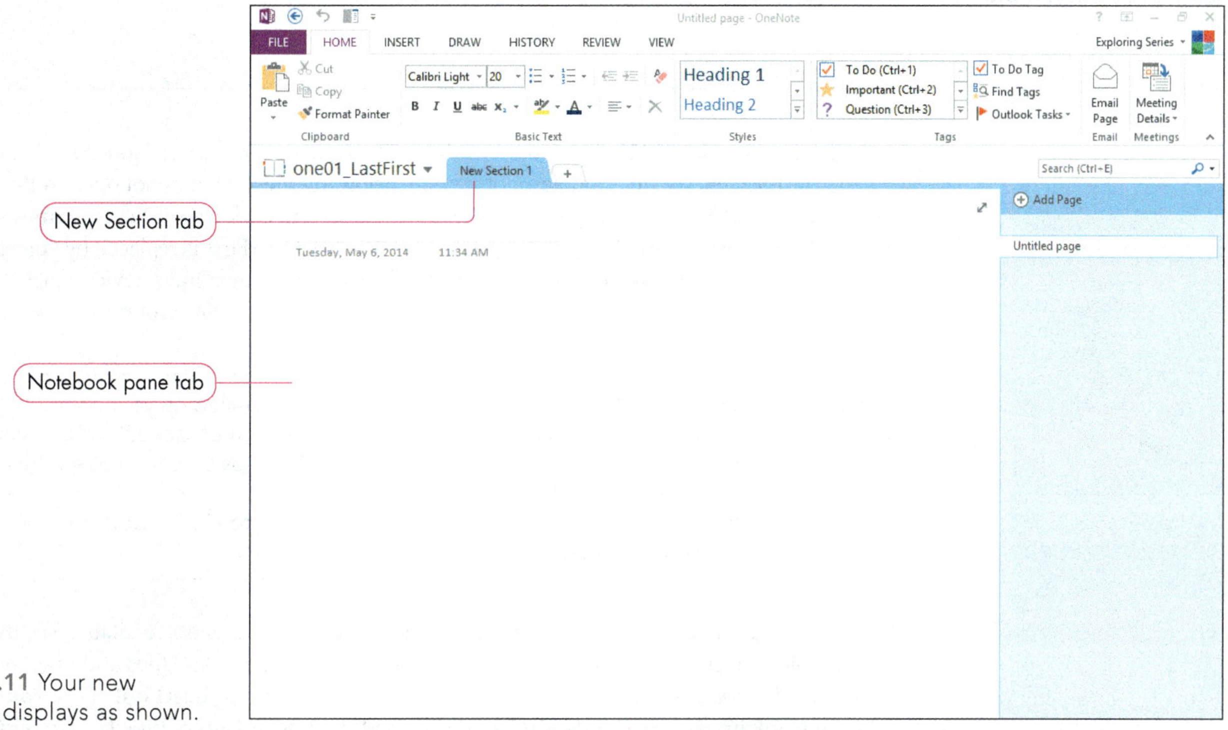

FIGURE 1.11 Your new notebook displays as shown.

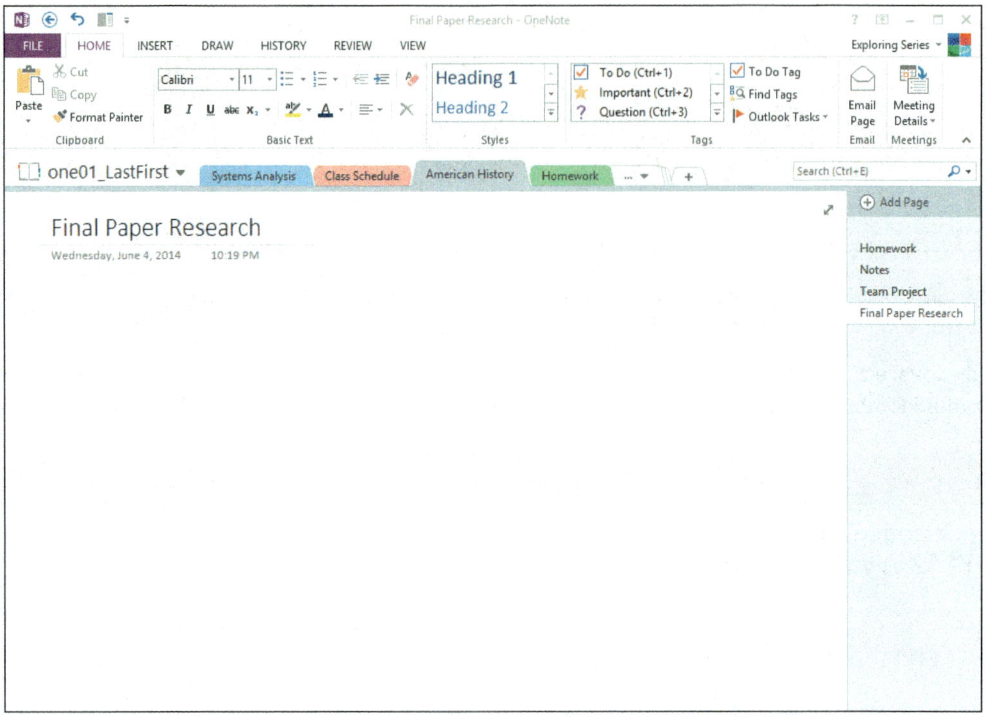

FIGURE 1.12 Six sections with pages are added to the notebook. When you create more sections than can display, a Section tab with an arrow provides access to the Section tabs that cannot be seen.

a. Click the **OneNote 2013** tile on the Windows 8 Start Screen. If the OneNote 2013 tile is not on the Start Screen, see the Troubleshooting note below. If OneNote does not open in Backstage view, click **FILE**. If necessary, on the left side of the screen, click **New**. Select **Computer**, type **one01_LastFirst** in the Notebook Name text box, where LastFirst is replaced by your Last and First name. Click **Create in a different folder**. Navigate to your storage device. Click **Create**. If a message asking you if you want to share the notebook displays, click **Not now**.

TROUBLESHOOTING: Microsoft OneNote 2013 must be installed on your computer to complete this exercise. If OneNote 2013 is installed, but the OneNote 2013 tile is not available on the Start screen, for Windows 8.1 click the All Apps button to open the Apps screen. Right-click the OneNote 2013 tile and pin to the Start screen. For Windows 8, right-click in a blank area of the screen, then click the All Apps button in the bottom right corner of the screen to get to the Apps screen.

b. On the Start screen, click the **Word 2013** tile. If the Word tile is not available, see the Troubleshooting information above. Navigate to your student data files and open *one01h1_CreateNotebook* and save the file as **one01h1CreateNotebook_LastFirst**. Type ***your name*** on a blank line under Hands-On Exercise 1, and then press **Enter**. Type the ***current date*** and then press **Enter** twice. Minimize Word.

TIP Finding Apps from the Start Screen

You can find any application from the Start screen by typing the name of the application. For instance, from the Start screen, type OneNote. A search pane will open with a link to OneNote.

c. Right-click the **New Section 1 tab** in OneNote, click **Rename**, and then type **Systems Analysis**.

d. Click the **Create a New Section tab**. Rename the new tab **Class Schedule**. Create a third tab and rename the tab **American History**. Add three more sections and name them **Homework**, **Speech Communication**, and **Algebra**.

e. Click the **Class Schedule Section tab**. Type **Monday, Wednesday, Friday** in the title area on the Untitled page. Click **Add Page**, above the Page tab. If necessary, click in the title area and name it **Tuesday, Thursday**.

f. Click the **Systems Analysis Section tab**. Type **Team Project** on the Untitled page, in the title area. **Add** four pages and title them **Homework**, **Final Paper Research**, **Class Schedule**, and **Notes**.

g. Add **Homework** and **Notes** pages to the Speech Communication and Algebra sections. Add **Homework, Notes**, **Team Project**, and **Final Paper Research** pages to the American History section.

h. Press the **Windows key** + **PrtScn** key. Maximize Word. Click below the information you typed at the top of the page, and then click **Paste** on the HOME tab, in the Clipboard section. Save and minimize Word.

STEP 2 ›› DELETE AND RENAME SECTIONS AND PAGES

After reviewing the notebook sections and pages, you realize you do not need separate pages for the Monday, Wednesday, Friday classes and Tuesday, Wednesday classes. You decide to delete the Monday, Wednesday, Friday classes page and the Tuesday, Wednesday classes page, and move the Course Calendar page to the Class Schedule section. After thinking a bit, you decide that each class section should have a separate homework page, so you will delete the Homework section. Refer to Figure 1.13 as you complete Step 2.

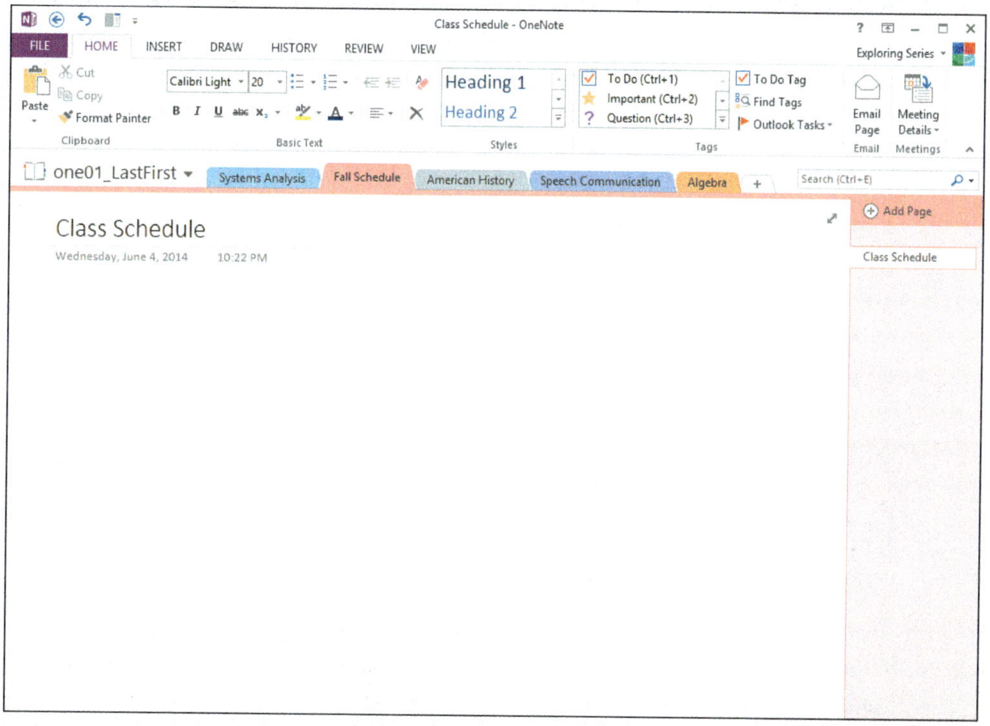

FIGURE 1.13 The Class Schedule Section tab is renamed and the Class Schedule page is moved into the renamed section.

a. Click the **Class Schedule Section tab**. Right-click the **Monday, Wednesday, Friday page tab**, and then click **Delete**. Right-click the **Tuesday, Thursday page tab**, and then click **Delete**.

TROUBLESHOOTING: If a message displays asking if you want to continue, click Yes.

b. Right-click the **Class Schedule Section tab**. Click **Rename**, and then type **Fall Schedule**, and then press **Enter**.

c. Click the **Systems Analysis Section tab**. Right-click the **Class Schedule Page tab**. Click **Move or Copy**. Make sure your *one01_LastFirst* notebook is selected in the Move or Copy Pages dialog box. Click the **expand (+) button** to the left of the notebook name, if necessary. Select the **Fall Schedule Section tab**, and then click **Move**.

The Class Schedule page will move to the Fall Schedule section.

d. Click the **Systems Analysis Section tab**. Right-click the **Homework Section tab**. Click **Delete**. Click **Yes**.

e. Click the **Fall Schedule Section tab**. Press the **Windows key** + **PrtScn** key. Maximize Word. Click below the last image you pasted into the document, and then click **Paste** on the HOME tab, in the Clipboard group. Save and minimize Word.

STEP 3 》 COPY A SECTION TO ANOTHER NOTEBOOK

Becky showed her new notebook to Jon Michaels. Jon asked her to set up a OneNote notebook for him using the exact same sections and pages. Becky has asked you to help her create Jon's notebook. Refer to Figure 1.14 as you complete Step 3.

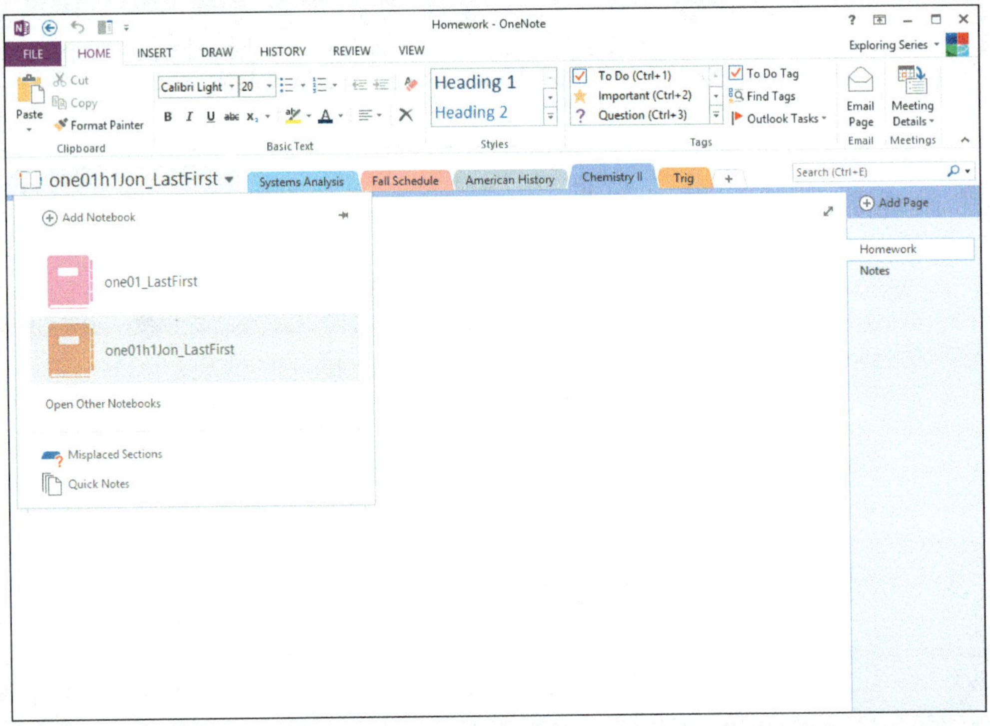

FIGURE 1.14 The Notebook Pane is pinned open.

a. Click the **FILE tab**, and then click **New**. Click **Computer**. Click **Create in a different folder**, navigate to your storage device, click **New folder**, name the folder **Exploring OneNote**, type **one01h1Jon_LastFirst** in the Notebook Name text box, and then click **Create**. If a message asking if you want to share the notebook displays, click **Not now**.

b. To the left of the first Section tab, click the **arrow** to open the Navigation pane to display all open notebooks. Click the **one01_LastFirst** to reopen the original notebook.

c. Right-click the **Systems Analysis Section tab**, in your *one01_LastFirst* notebook. Click **Move or Copy**. Select ***one01h1Jon_LastFirst***, and then click **Copy**. Use the same method to copy the remaining section tabs to *one01h1Jon_LastFirst*.

d. Click **one01h1Jon_LastFirst** in the Navigation pane. Delete the **New Section 1 Section tab**, in the *one01h1Jon_LastFirst*. Whereas Jon shares most of your classes, instead of Speech Communication, he is taking Chemistry II. **Rename** the Speech Communication section as **Chemistry II**. Jon is taking Trigonometry instead of Algebra, so rename the Algebra Section tab **Trig**.

e. Click the Notebook Pane arrow to open the Notebook Pane.

TIP Pin the Notebook Pane

To keep the Notebook Pane open, click the Pin Notebook Pane to Side icon in the top right corner of the pane. To close a pinned Notebook Pane, click the pin icon again.

f. Press the **Windows key** + **PrtScn** key. Maximize Word. Click below the last image you pasted into the document, and then click **Paste** on the HOME tab, in the Clipboard group. Save and minimize Word.

g. Open the **Navigation Pane**. Right-click **one01h1Jon_LastFirst**, and then click **Close This Notebook**.

STEP 4 » REARRANGE SECTIONS AND PAGES

Becky has decided to rearrange the sections in order of her classes, Monday, Wednesday, Friday classes first, and then in order of scheduled time, and then Tuesday, Thursday classes. Refer to Figure 1.15 as you complete Step 4.

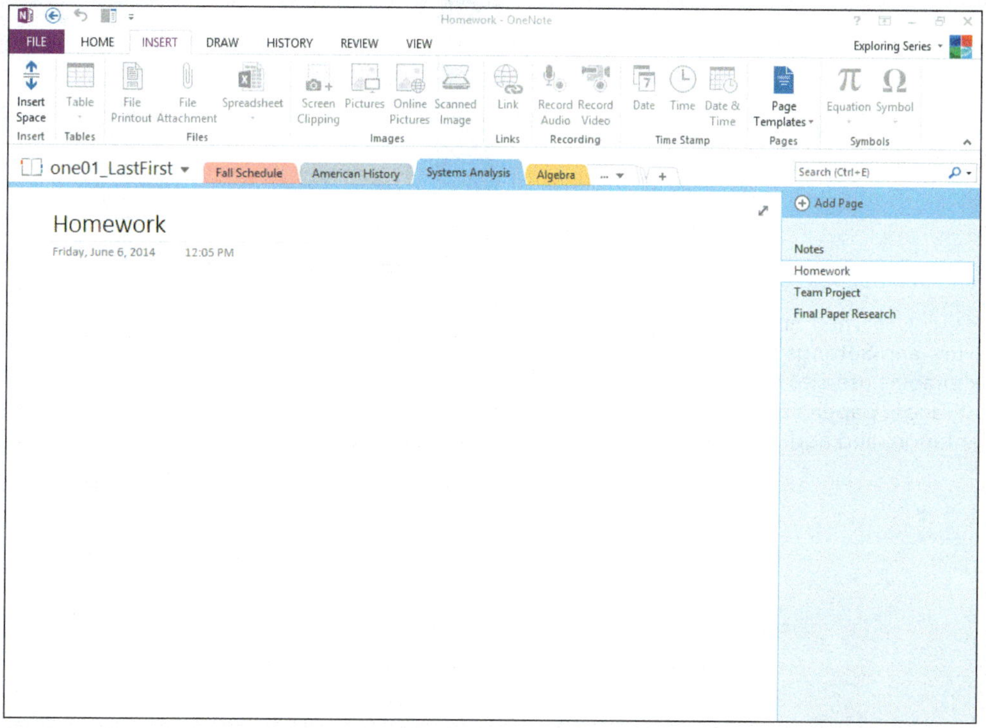

FIGURE 1.15 Sections and pages are rearranged.

a. Click the **American History Section tab**, hold the left mouse key and drag the tab to the left until a small down arrow displays above and to the left of the first section tab. Release the left mouse button. Use the same technique to rearrange the sections in the order listed below:

American History
Systems Analysis
Algebra
Speech Communication

b. Drag the **Fall Schedule section tab** to the left of the American History section tab.

c. On the **Systems Analysis section tab**, click on the **Notes page tab**. Hold down the left mouse button and drag the tab to the top of the list.

d. Click the **Homework page tab**. Drag the tab below the Notes page tab.

   The pages should be in Notes, Homework, Team Project, and Final Paper Research order.

e. Press the **Windows key** + **PrtScn** key. Maximize Word. Click below the last image you pasted into the document, and then click **Paste** on the HOME tab, in the Clipboard group. Save and minimize Word.

STEP 5 » ADD A FOOTER, PRINT A SECTION, AND SEND A SECTION

Becky has decided to print the Systems Analysis section for easy reference when she does not have access to her computer. She has decided that she needs page numbers, in case the pages are dropped and are no longer in order. Refer to Figures 1.16 and 1.17 as you complete Step 5.

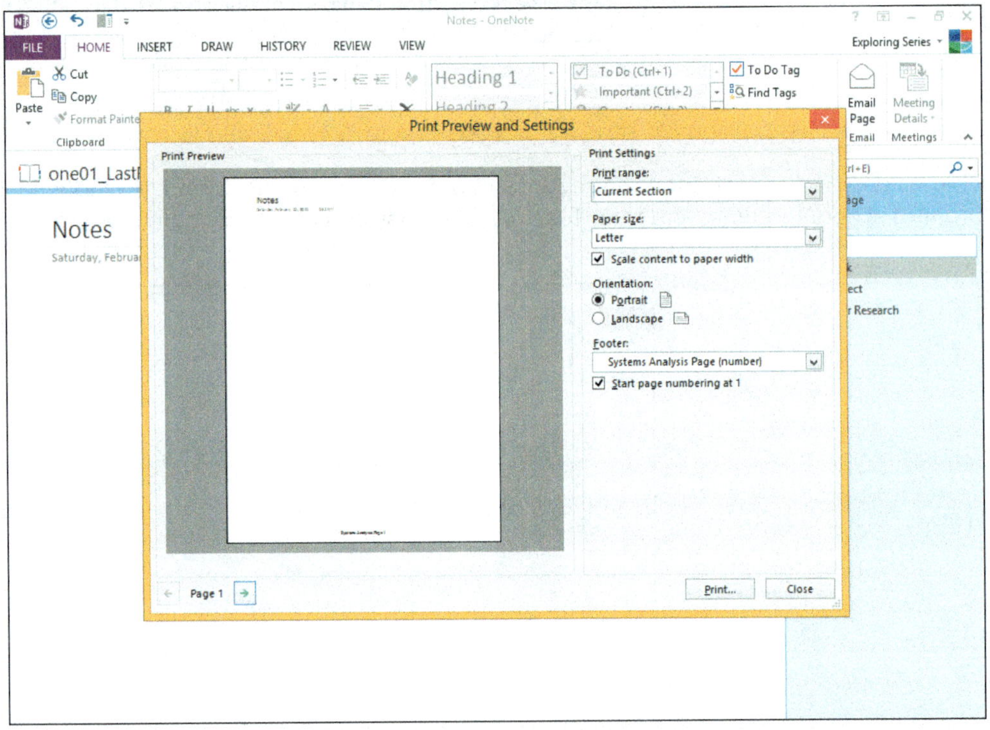

FIGURE 1.16 The Print Preview and Settings dialog box enables users to set the print range, paper size, page orientation, and add a footer.

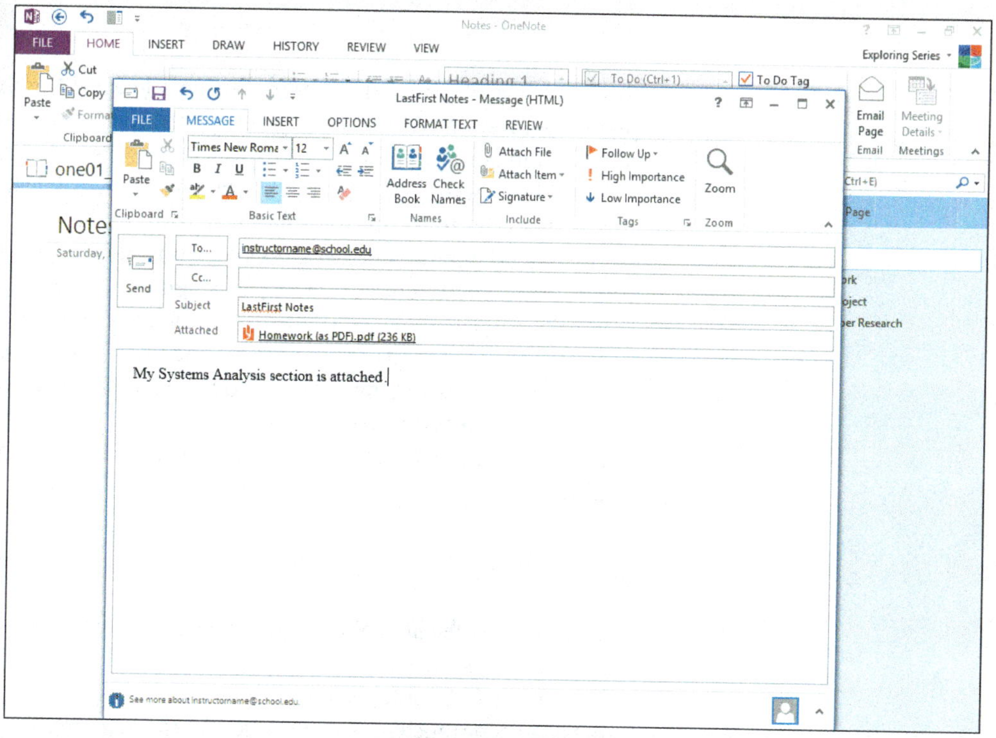

FIGURE 1.17 Using Outlook, you can send a section as an attachment to an e-mail.

a. Click the **Systems Analysis section tab**, and then click the **FILE tab**. Click **Print**, and then click **Print Preview**. Select **Current Section**, in the Print range. Make sure Paper size is set to **Letter**, and the **Scale content to paper width** is checked.

b. If necessary, select **Portrait** for the Orientation. Make sure the Footer selection is **Systems Analysis Page (number)**, and **Start page numbering at 1** is checked.

c. Use the arrow buttons at the bottom of the Print Preview pane to scroll through all pages in the section.

d. Press the **Windows key** + **PrtScn** key. Maximize Word. Click below the last image you pasted into the document, and then click **Paste** on the HOME tab, in the Clipboard group. Save and minimize Word. If your instructor has instructed you to print this page, click **Print**. Otherwise, click **Close**.

e. Click the **FILE tab**. Click **Send**. Click **Send as PDF**.

f. Type *your instructor's email address* in the **TO box** in the email address form. Change the Subject line to **LastFirst Notes**.

g. Type **My Systems Analysis section is attached**. in the message box.

h. Press the **Windows key** + **PrtScn** key. Maximize Word. Click below the last image you pasted into the document, and then click **Paste** on the HOME tab, in the Clipboard group.

i. Save and close Word. Close OneNote. If directed by your instructor, click **Send**. Otherwise, close the e-mail window without saving or sending. Submit the Word document as directed by your instructor.

Add Content to OneNote 2013

Research has shown that different learners learn differently. There are auditory learners, people who learn better hearing information, visual learners who learn better by seeing information, and kinesthetic learners, who have to actually use the information or perform a task to learn well. OneNote works equally well for all learning types. Auditory learners can use the recorder to record their notes verbally so that they can listen to them. The actions of reading aloud and then hearing the recording played back both help the auditory learner. By using formatting to change colors, highlight, and change font sizes and fonts, visual learners can better learn the information. Typing their notes or, if they have a tablet, handwriting their notes helps kinesthetic learners remember lesson material. Regardless of which learning style you possess, OneNote lets you learn in the best way for your style, because you can add color to text (visual), use the pen and drawing tools to create small sketches, mindmaps, and illustrations (kinesthetic), or record yourself reading your notes aloud to listen to later (auditory).

Add Notes

One of the best features of OneNote is that you can add so many different types of content. In this section, you will learn how to add notes, screen clips, Internet information, photos, and files to a OneNote 2013 notebook. OneNote allows you to add notes by typing, or writing if you are using a tablet or touch screen, anywhere in the Page area. To add notes, simply click on the page below the page title and date, then start typing. A ***container*** is added to hold the text you type. Sometimes, though, you need to add more than just typed or written notes. See Figure 1.18.

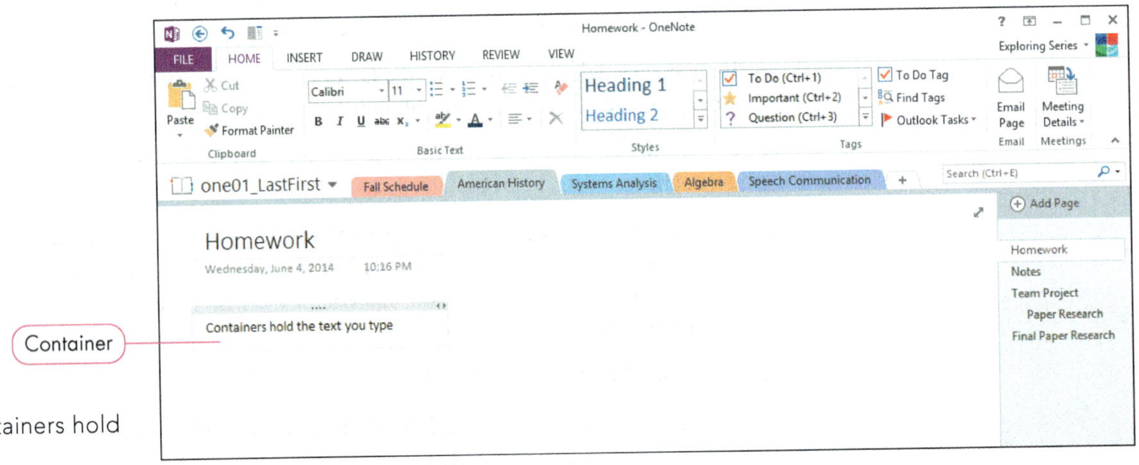

FIGURE 1.18 Containers hold the text you type.

Create Screen Clips

STEP 1 »

Occasionally, you may need to have an image of content on your screen. A screen clip or ***screenshot*** is a snapshot of your screen that creates an image that can be saved or pasted into Microsoft applications. There are three basic ways to capture screen clips or screenshots:

- Snipping Tool for Windows 8.1 desktop.
- Windows key + Print Screen for Windows 8.1 Start screen.
- Send to OneNote.

The ***Snipping Tool*** can only be used when you are working in the desktop environment. To make the Snipping Tool easily accessible on the desktop, add it to the desktop taskbar:

1. Open the Windows 8.1 Start screen.
2. Click in a blank area and start typing Snipping Tool.
3. In the list that pops up, right-click on the Snipping Tool.
4. Click Pin to Taskbar.

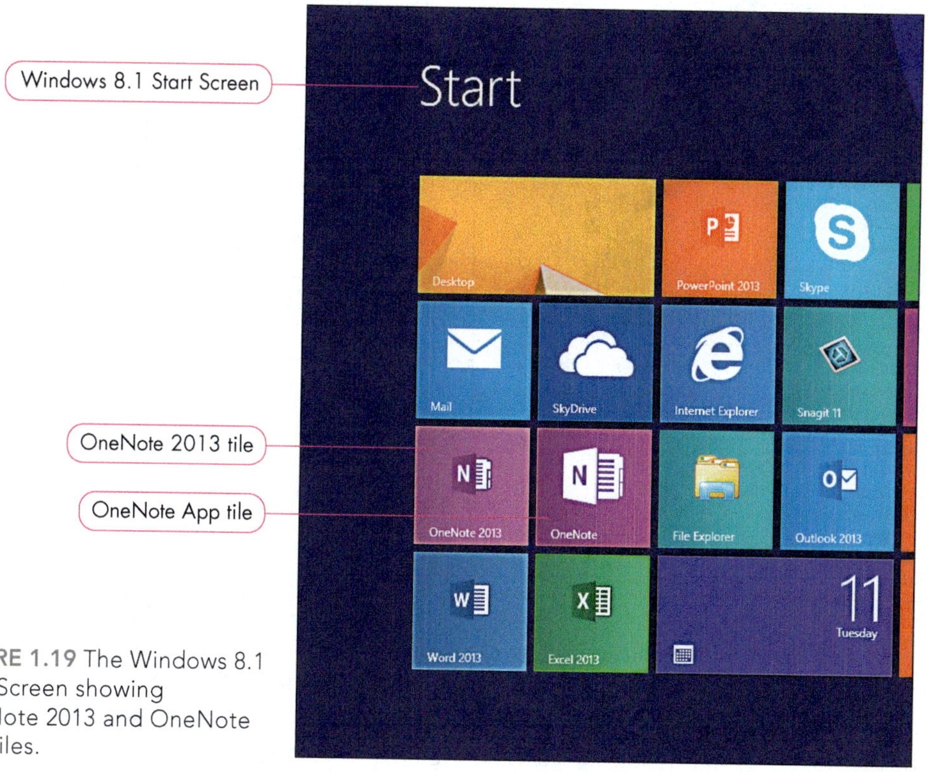

FIGURE 1.19 The Windows 8.1 Start Screen showing OneNote 2013 and OneNote App tiles.

To add the Snipping Tool to your Start screen:

1. Right-click on the Snipping Tool tile.
2. Click Pin to Start.

Because the Snipping Tool only works from the desktop, it cannot be used to take a screenshot of the Windows 8.1 Start screen. Without purchasing specialized image capture software, there is only one way to get a screen clip of the Start screen: On your keyboard, to the left and right of your spacebar, there is a Windows or Start key. Some keyboards will only have the Windows or Start key on the left side of the spacebar. If you hold down the Windows key and press the PrtScn key, the monitor will briefly flash while Windows 8.1 takes a screenshot. The screenshot of the Start screen is stored in active memory and is saved to the Pictures Library in a folder named *Screenshots*. The file will be saved with a default file name of Screenshot (#) where # is replaced by a number. Each time you take a screenshot, the number will increment to the next higher number. You can navigate to the Screenshots folder in the Pictures Library, rename the image file, and move it to the appropriate location. Because the image is in active memory until another screenshot is captured, it can also be pasted into a Word document, PowerPoint presentation, Excel worksheet, or OneNote notebook.

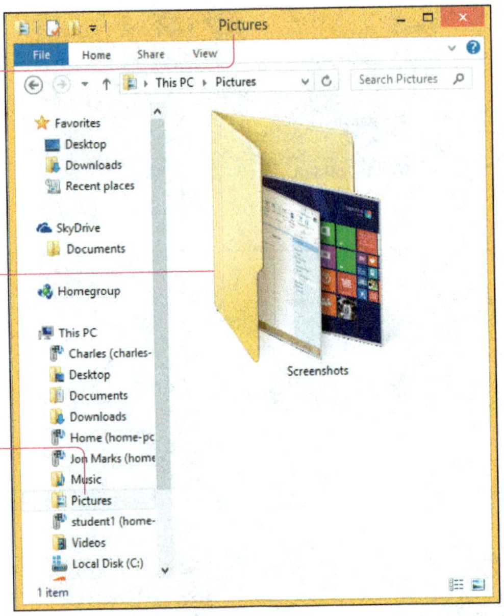

FIGURE 1.20 Screenshots created with the Windows key + PrtScn key combination are saved in the Screenshots folder in the Pictures Library.

When you open OneNote, a Send to OneNote button is added to the Taskbar. The Send to OneNote button allows you to use OneNote to take an image of a screen or Web site and send it to OneNote. A dialog box allows you to specify exactly what is sent and which section page it is sent to. To send a screen capture using Send to OneNote:

1. Open OneNote.
2. With the image you wish to capture on the screen, click the Send to OneNote button on the Taskbar.
3. Click Screen Clipping (S).
4. Use the mouse to select a region on the screen to clip.
5. Select a Notebook, Section, and Page where you want to send the clipping.
6. Click Send to Selected Location.

The image will be inserted into the selected section or page in OneNote. From this location, you can right-click on the image and save it as a .png image file. Navigate to the location to which you wish to save the image, type the file name of the image, and then click Save.

Capture Internet Information

STEP 2»

Capturing information from the Internet is an important part of research for writing class papers. Using the Send to OneNote button, there are three options to capture information:

- Screen Clipping (S).
- Send to OneNote (D).
- New Quick Note (N).

FIGURE 1.21 Send to OneNote options enable the user to specify what will be sent to OneNote.

The Send to OneNote (D) option publishes an open file from a desktop application to your OneNote page. For instance, if you have a PowerPoint presentation open on the desktop, the Send to OneNote button sends images of every slide in the presentation to the selected page in OneNote. To use the Send to OneNote Screen Clipping (S) option to send a clip of the open file, follow the instructions in the previous section for capturing a screen image. To send the entire file to OneNote, use the Send to OneNote (D) option:

1. Open the file you wish to send to OneNote (example: Word, PowerPoint, Excel).
2. Click Send to OneNote in the Taskbar.
3. Select the Send to OneNote (D) option.
4. Select the notebook and section to which you wish to send the file.
5. Click OK.

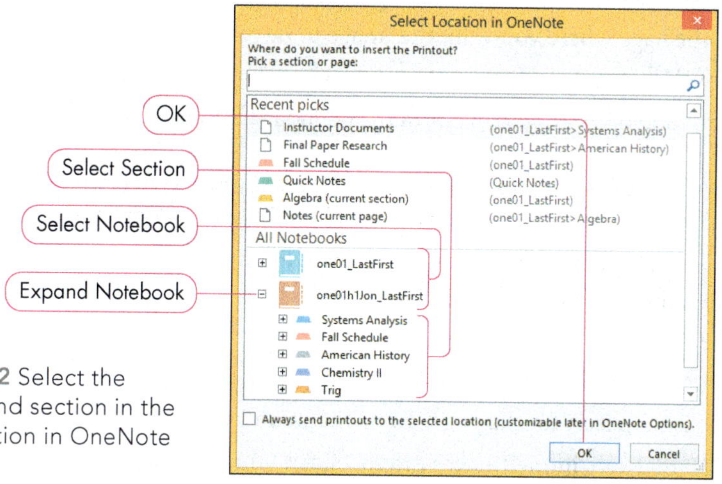

FIGURE 1.22 Select the notebook and section in the Select Location in OneNote dialog box.

The New Quick Note (N) option opens a text screen. Type the note, and then click the X in the top right corner of the text screen. The ***quick note***, a note that has not been placed into a specific page, will be placed in the Quick Notes section, available in the Notebooks pane. To create a note and insert it into a specific notebook page:

1. Click Send to OneNote.
2. Click New Quick Note (N).
3. Type the note in the Quick Note text screen.
4. Select the text you typed.
5. Right-click the selected text.
6. Click Copy.
7. Navigate to the page where you want to insert the note.
8. Right-click on the page, and then click Paste.

An alternate method is to select and copy information or images on the Web page and then paste them into OneNote.

Insert a Link

Sometimes the information you locate on the Web is too lengthy to insert into your notes. In this instance, you can link to the Web page, rather than inserting a full document or image. A Web page link can be inserted into the document by using the following steps:

1. In your browser, navigate to the Web site.
2. Copy the URL in the browser address bar.
3. In OneNote, on the INSERT tab, in the Links group, click Link.
4. Type the text that will display in the link.
5. Paste the URL in the Address textbox.
6. Click OK.

You can also link to a location in OneNote by following these steps:

1. On the INSERT tab, in the Links group, click Link.
2. Click the expand button (+) to the left of the appropriate notebook.
3. Click the expand button (+) to the left of the appropriate section.
4. Select the page to which you wish to link.
5. Click OK.

Paste or Insert a Photo

STEP 3 To paste a photo, it must first be stored in the computer's clipboard, a section of memory set aside to hold temporary items. Taking a screenshot puts the screen image into the clipboard. To paste a photo into OneNote:

1. Click on the page where you want the image to be placed.
2. On the HOME tab, in the Clipboard group, click the top half of the Paste button.

An alternate method of pasting items from the clipboard is to use the Ctrl+V keyboard combination.

Attaching a photo inserts a link to the file on your storage device. Clicking that link then opens the file. To attach a photo located on your hard drive, USB, or other storage location:

1. On the INSERT tab, in the Images group, click Pictures.
2. Navigate to the location where the file is saved.
3. Select the file.
4. Click Insert.

The image is inserted into the page. To insert an online photo:

1. On the INSERT tab, in the Images group, click Online Pictures.
2. Select Office.com Clip Art, Bing Image Search, or your OneDrive, if you are logged in to OneDrive.
3. Type keywords into the appropriate text box.
4. Press Enter.
5. Select one or more images.
6. Click Insert.

To select more than one image, hold down the Ctrl key while selecting. If you have the OneNote Mobile app installed on your Smartphone or tablet, you can use the camera to take a photo and add it to your notes. To learn more about using OneNote Mobile on your phone, visit **http://www.windowsphone.com/en-US/how-to/wp8/apps/use-onenote-mobile**.

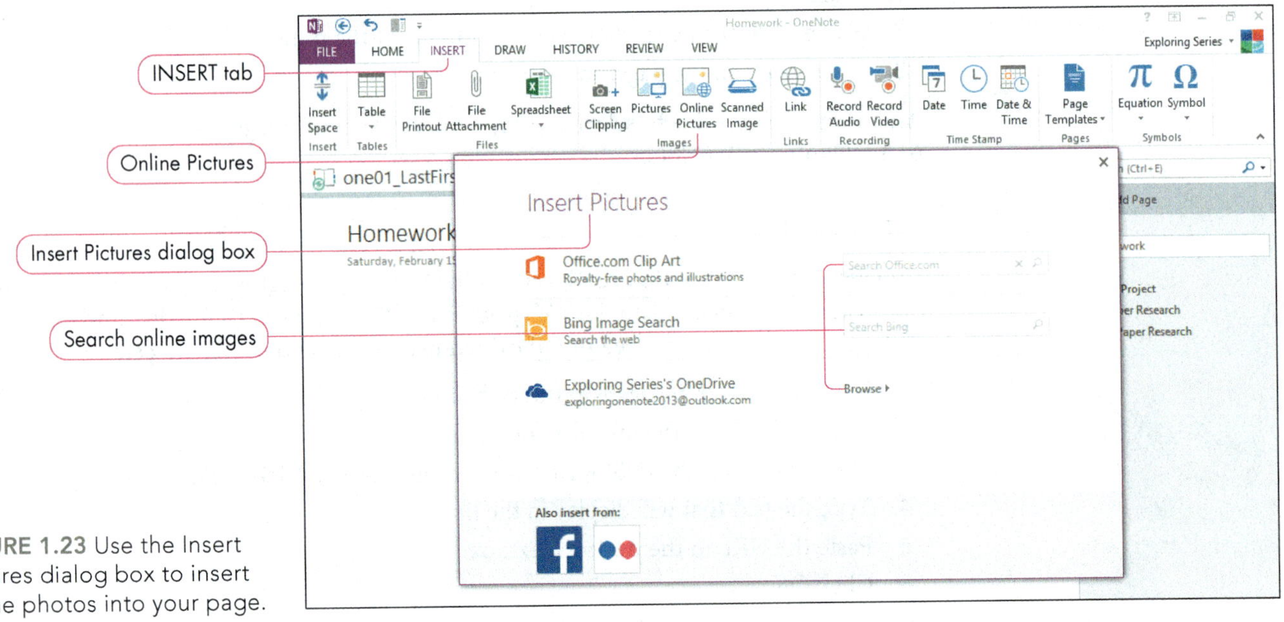

FIGURE 1.23 Use the Insert Pictures dialog box to insert online photos into your page.

Convert Text from an Image

STEP 4

One of the exciting features of OneNote is the ability to convert text from images. What this means is that instead of taking time to take notes from a whiteboard or chalkboard during a class or business lecture, you can take a photo of the notes on the board with a digital camera, or you could use the built-in camera in your mobile device to take a still image, and then use OneNote's built-in ***optical character recognition (OCR)*** capability to convert the image to text notes that can be annotated or tagged as needed. Optical character recognition software is a computer program that converts text in scanned documents and photographs into text.

To convert an image containing text into text, do the following:

1. Insert the scanned image or photo into your notes page area.
2. Right-click on the image, and then select Copy Text from Picture.
3. Paste the text from the image into a new container on the same or a new notes page.

The converted text pasted into the page can be edited and formatted in the same way as text you typed into the page. For best results, crop the image to include only the part of the image you desire to convert to text. If you do not have a graphics program, you can do this in Paint, an accessory application that comes with Windows, or in Word. After cropping the image in Word, right-click the image, and then click Save as Picture. In the File Save dialog box, navigate to the folder where you wish to save the image, select the image file type, type a filename for the image, and then click Save.

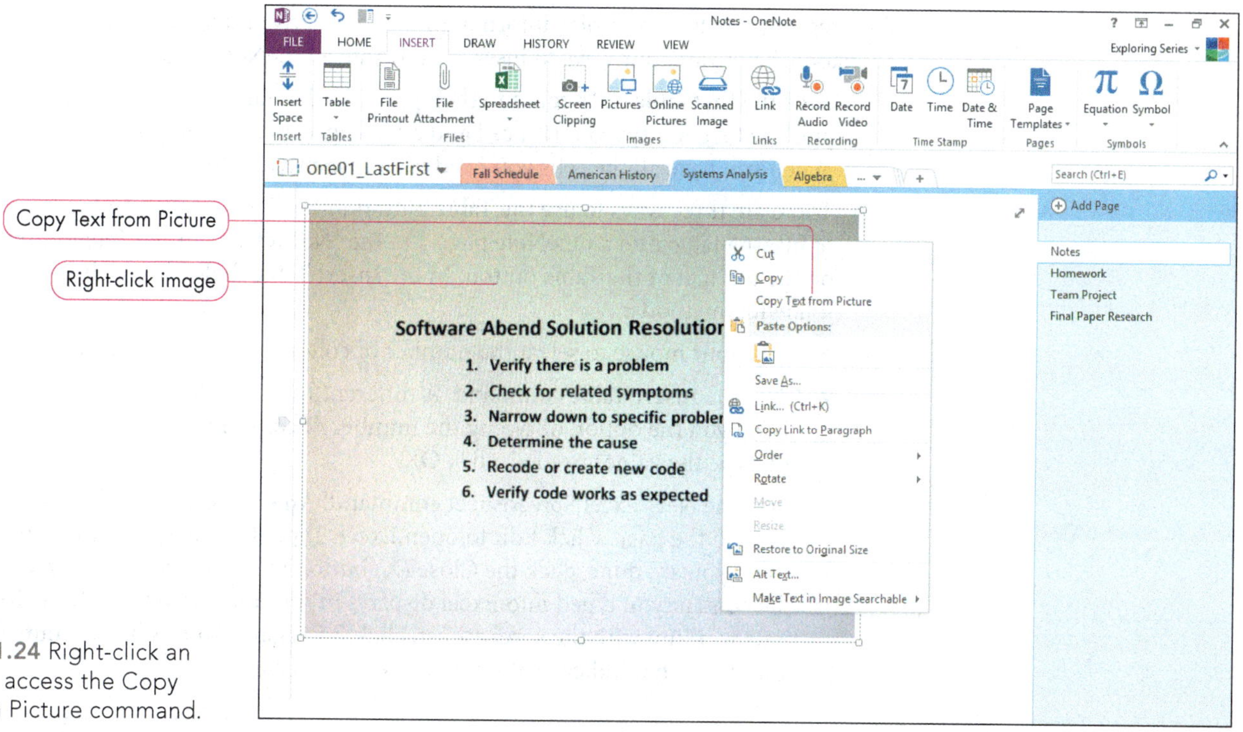

FIGURE 1.24 Right-click an image to access the Copy Text from Picture command.

Insert a Scanned Image

There may be occasions when you need to scan images or text content into OneNote. For instance, if you miss a class, you can scan a classmate's notes into OneNote instead of typing them. Before scanning an image into OneNote, be sure to place the image to be scanned on the scanner. To scan an image into OneNote:

1. In the Images group on the INSERT tab, click Scanned Image.
2. In the Insert Picture from Scanner or Camera dialog box, select the device.
3. Select the resolution.
4. Click Insert. If you are inserting from the scanner, the image will display on your page.

Attach a File

Attaching files such as text documents, file printouts, spreadsheets, screen clippings, pictures, scanned images, or audio or video recordings is done on the INSERT tab. To attach a text file, database, or PDF document, in the Files group, click File Attachment. Navigate to where the file is saved on your hard drive, select the file, and then click Insert. In the Insert File dialog box, select whether to attach the file or insert a printout.

There is a difference between attached and inserted content. Inserted content displays in full on the screen similar to a printout of the file. Attached content shows a file icon and the file name. To see the content that is attached, you have to open the file. To open an attached file, select one of the following methods:

- Right-click on the file, and then click Open.
- Double-click the file.

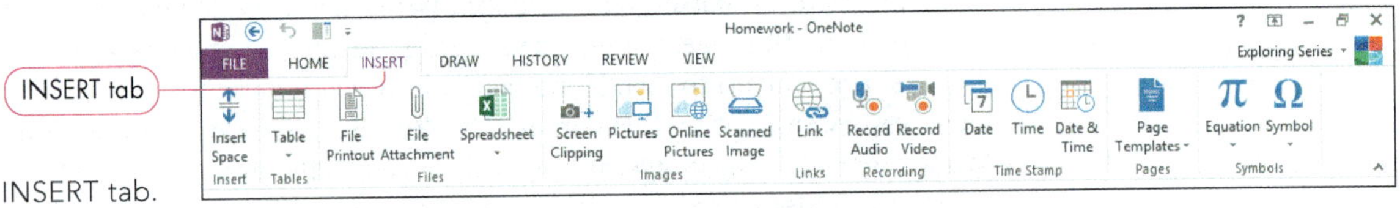

FIGURE 1.25 The INSERT tab.

Create a Table

STEP 5》 Tables make it possible to display information in an orderly and logical manner that is easily understood. There are four ways to insert a table into a OneNote page:

- Type the first table cell's content, then press the Tab key. OneNote automatically puts the text you typed into a cell and adds another cell to the right of the first. When you have all the cells you need for a row, press Enter to start a new table row.
- There are three ways to use the Table button in the Tables group on the INSERT tab to insert a table into a OneNote page. On the INSERT tab, in the Tables group, click on the top half of the Table button. In the Insert Table dialog box, select one of the following methods:
  - Drag your mouse to select the number of columns and rows you need.
  - Click the Insert Table command. A different Insert Table dialog box displays, giving you the option of typing the number of columns and rows you need. After you type the values needed, click OK.
  - Click the New Excel Spreadsheet command. An embedded Excel worksheet displays on the page. Click Edit to open Excel. Type the values and text you need. When you are done, click the Close (X) button in the top right corner. Click Save. The content you typed into Excel displays in the embedded worksheet. To continue working with the spreadsheet, click Edit again. To finish, click outside the dotted line that indicates the spreadsheet is selected.

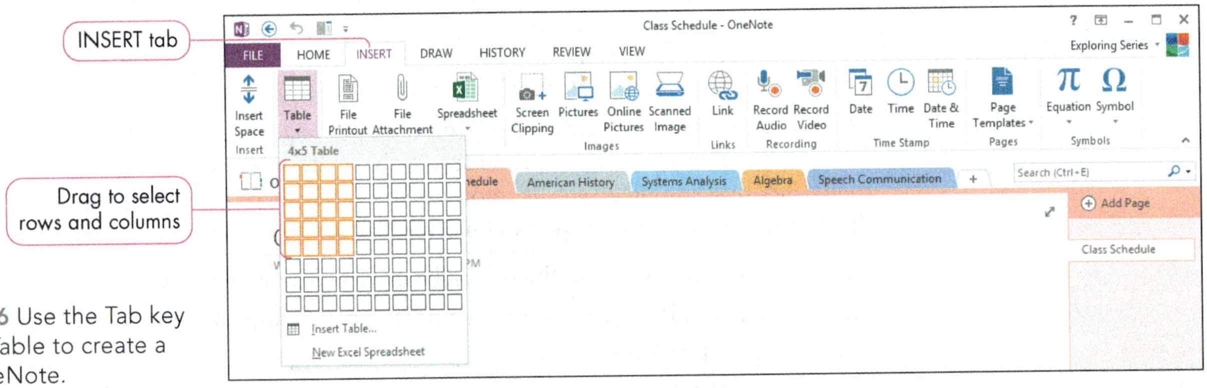

FIGURE 1.26 Use the Tab key or INSERT Table to create a table in OneNote.

Add a Calculation

There may be times in your note taking that you will need to add a calculation. Whereas you could open a calculator app, it is not necessary. OneNote allows you to type calculations directly on your page. To add a calculation:

1. Click on the page where you want to add the calculation.
2. Type the calculation, ending it with an equal sign (=).
3. Press Enter.

Table 1.2 shows the standard math symbols used in Microsoft OneNote 2013 for mathematic operators.

TABLE 1.2 Math Symbols

Symbol	Operation
*	Multiplication
/	Division
–	Subtraction
+	Addition
^	Exponentiation (to the power of)
( )	Parentheses are used to group values in equations

Example: (2*8)+(3–2)+23=

When this example is keyed into OneNote, the application automatically calculates the answer to be 40. For more complex calculations, click on the INSERT tab, and in the Symbols group, click the bottom half of the Equation button to display common mathematical formulas available for inserting into the page, including Area of Circle, Binomial Theorem, Expansion of a Sum, Fourier Series, and Pythagorean Theorem formulas. Below the formulas, you can click the Insert New Equation command to access the contextual tab EQUATION TOOLS DESIGN. Alternatively, you can click the top half of the Equation button to open the EQUATION TOOLS DESIGN tab.

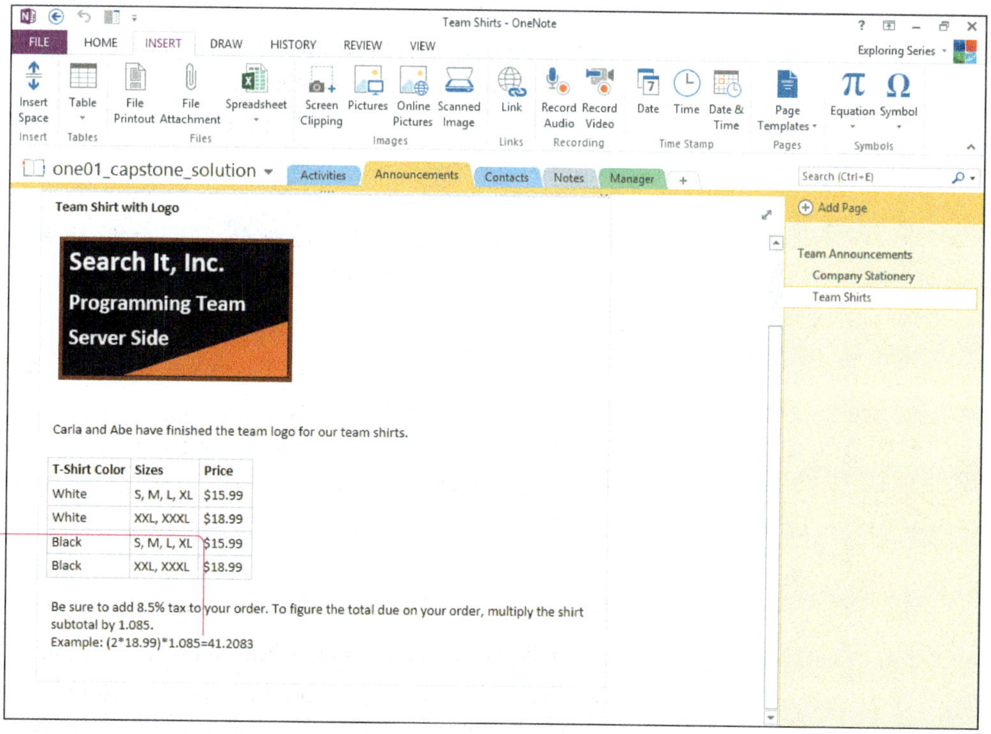

OneNote calculates equation

FIGURE 1.27 Type an equation followed by the equal sign and OneNote will calculate it.

Add Audio or Video to a Page

There are two ways you can add an audio clip to a OneNote page:

- You can record an audio file from within OneNote. To do this, you will need a computer-compatible microphone or a headset with a microphone. The Record Audio button is in the Recording group on the INSERT tab.
- You can attach an existing audio file to a page using the File Attachment command in the Files group on the INSERT tab.

To record a video file to add to a notes page, you must have a webcam on your computer or tablet. This is a helpful tool for recording meetings with business associates or class project teammates. The Record Video command is located in the Recording group on the INSERT tab. Attaching a video is accomplished the same way as attaching an audio file.

Integrate Content from Office

STEP 6》 Most Microsoft applications can be integrated with each other, and OneNote is no exception. As previously noted, using the INSERT tab, you can attach files. You can also use the INSERT tab to insert a file printout. This prints the document into your notebook. You can also send file contents to OneNote using the Send to OneNote tile. This can be helpful when your instructor sends you a file with information you would like to incorporate directly into your notes.

To insert a file printout, follow these steps:

1. Navigate to the page where you want the file printout inserted.
2. Click to place your pointer at the page location where you want the file inserted.
3. On the INSERT tab, in the Files group, click File Printout.
4. Navigate to your storage media.
5. Select the file.
6. Click Insert.

The file will be "printed" to the OneNote page. This can be done with Word, Excel, and PowerPoint files.

The Spreadsheet command in the Files group allows you to include an existing spreadsheet or to create a new Excel spreadsheet. To include an Existing Excel Spreadsheet:

1. On the INSERT tab, in the Files group, click the arrow beneath the Spreadsheet button.
2. Click Existing Excel Spreadsheet.
3. Navigate to your student data files.
4. Select the Excel file.
5. Click Insert.
6. In the Insert File dialog box, select one of the three options: Attach File, Insert Spreadsheet, or Insert a Chart or Table.

To create a new spreadsheet:

1. On the INSERT tab, in the Files group, click the arrow beneath the Spreadsheet button.
2. Click New Excel Spreadsheet.
3. Click the Edit button in the spreadsheet window to open Excel.
4. Create the spreadsheet.
5. Close Excel.

Alternatively, you can use Send to OneNote to send Office files to your OneNote page. With a Word, Excel, or PowerPoint file open and active on the desktop, follow these steps:

1. Click the Send to OneNote button on the taskbar.
2. Click the center button titled Send to OneNote (D) (the image changes depending on which type of file is open, and if you are in OneNote, the image is grayed out).

3. In the Select Location in OneNote dialog box, expand the appropriate notebook.
4. Expand the appropriate section.
5. Select the page.
6. Click OK.

The document, spreadsheet, or presentation will be printed to OneNote in its entirety. Depending on the application you are using, Word, Excel, or PowerPoint, the image in the Send to OneNote (D) image will differ. If you are in OneNote, the Send to OneNote (D) button is grayed out.

Send to OneNote (D)

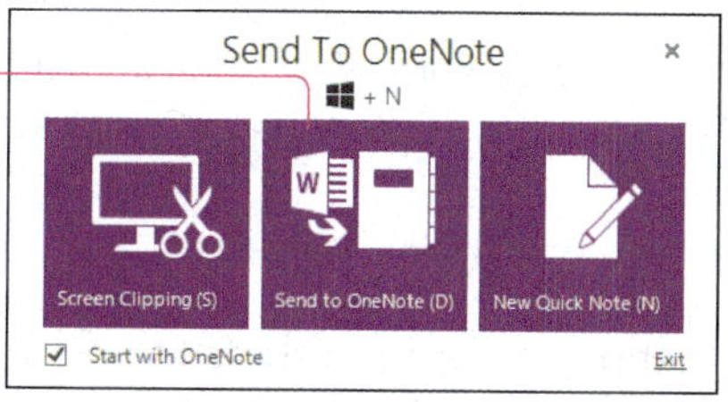

FIGURE 1.28 The Send to OneNote (D) image changes depending on the application from which you are sending content.

Quick Concepts

1. When would you paste an image rather than insert an image into your page? ***p. 22***
2. Explain how to capture a screenshot to add to a OneNote notebook page. ***p. 18***
3. What advantage does converting an image to text provide as a student? ***p. 23***
4. Give three examples of when might you need to key a calculation into a OneNote page? ***p. 25***

Hands-On Exercises

2 Add Content to OneNote 2013

Now that Becky's notebook is set up, you will help her add notes, screen clips, a link, and an illustration. You will help her convert text in an image to text in a note page and attach a file, create a table, insert an audio file, and add a calculation to a section.

Skills covered: Add Notes and Insert Screen Clips • Insert Links and Capture Information from the Internet • Insert and Paste Photos • Convert Text from an Image to Text and Attach a File • Integrate Office Files • Create a Table and Add a Calculation

STEP 1 ❯❯ ADD NOTES AND INSERT SCREEN CLIPS

In this section, Becky needs to add team project information, and screen shots to her class notebook. You will help her add notes to the notebook created in Exercise 1. Refer to Figures 1.29 and 1.30 as you complete Step 1.

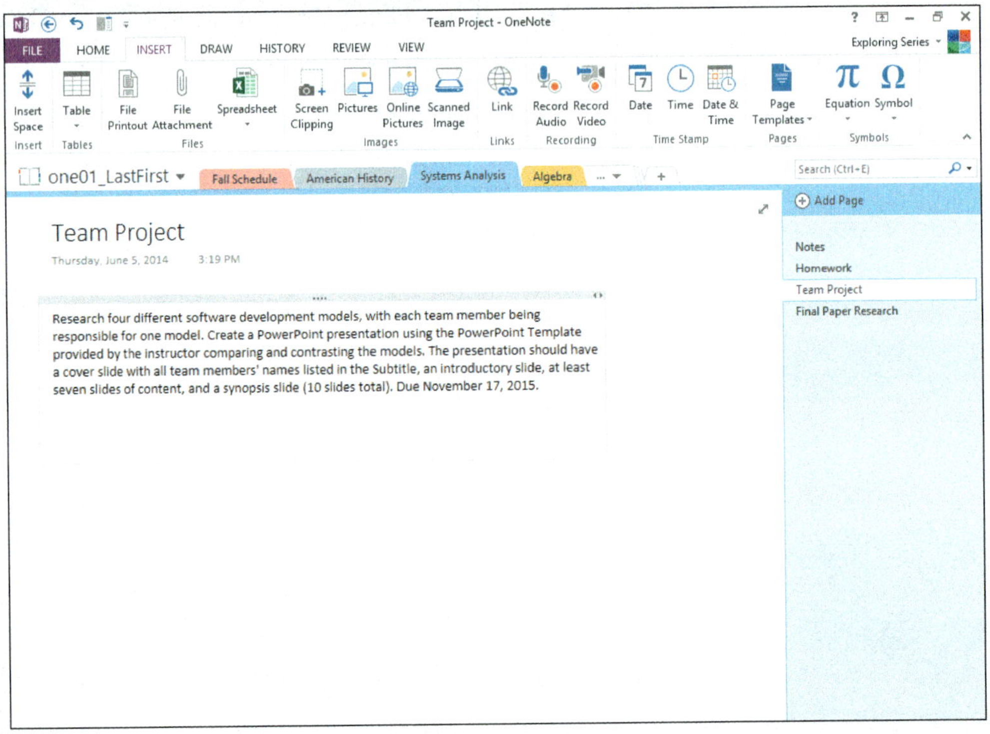

FIGURE 1.29 Content is added to the Team Project page.

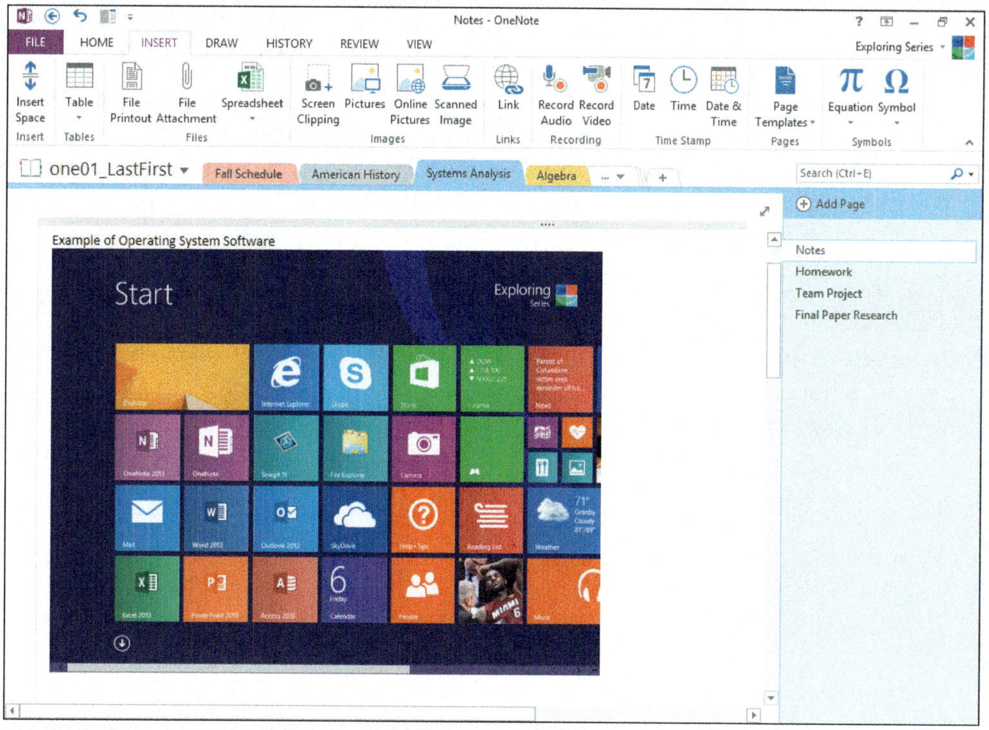

FIGURE 1.30 A screenshot of the Start screen is pasted into the Systems Analysis Notes page.

a. Open **OneNote 2013**. If necessary, Click the **FILE tab**, click **Open**, and then select your **one01_LastFirst** notebook.

b. Open **Word**. Navigate to your student data files. Open **one01h2_AddNotes** Type **your name**, below the subtitle, and then press **Enter**. Type the **current date**. Press **Enter** twice. Save the Word file as **one01h2_AddNotes_LastFirst**. Minimize Word.

c. Click on the **Systems Analysis section tab** in OneNote. Click the **Team Project Page tab**. Click below the title, and then type the following:

   Research four different software development models, with each team member being responsible for one model. Create a PowerPoint presentation using the PowerPoint Template provided by the instructor comparing and contrasting the models. The presentation should have a cover slide with all team members' names listed in the Subtitle, an introductory slide, at least seven slides of content, and a synopsis slide (10 slides total). Due November 17, 2016. Press **Enter** twice.

d. Navigate to your **Windows 8 Start Screen**. Use the **Windows key** + **PrtScn** key combination to capture a screen shot of the Start Screen.

e. Return to OneNote. On the **Systems Analysis Section tab**, below the date on the **Notes** page, type **Example of Operating System Software**, and then press **Enter**. Press **Ctrl+V** to paste the image into your OneNote page.

f. If you have the Snipping Tool pinned to your desktop taskbar, skip to step h. If you do not have the Snipping Tool pinned to your desktop taskbar, navigate to your **Start Screen**.

TIP Are you using Windows 8 or 8.1?

Steps for opening the All Apps screen in Windows 8 differ, depending on the version of Windows 8. For Windows 8.1, use the All Apps button to navigate to the All Apps page. For Windows 8, right-click on a blank area of the Start Screen, then click the All Apps button at the bottom right corner.

g. Locate the **Snipping Tool tile**. Right-click the **tile**, and then click **Pin to Taskbar** at the bottom of the screen. Navigate back to **OneNote**.

h. Click the **Snipping Tool icon** on the taskbar. Click the **New arrow**, click **Full-screen Snip**, and then click anywhere on your screen to take a screen snip. Click **Edit**. Click **Copy**. Maximize Word. **Paste** the snip below the date. Save and minimize Word. Close the Snipping Tool without saving.

STEP 2 » CAPTURE INTERNET INFORMATION AND INSERT A LINK

Becky needs to add research information for her American History research project to her notebook. In this section, you will help her add a URL link to the Final Paper Research page and add information from the Internet. Refer to Figure 1.31 as you complete Step 2.

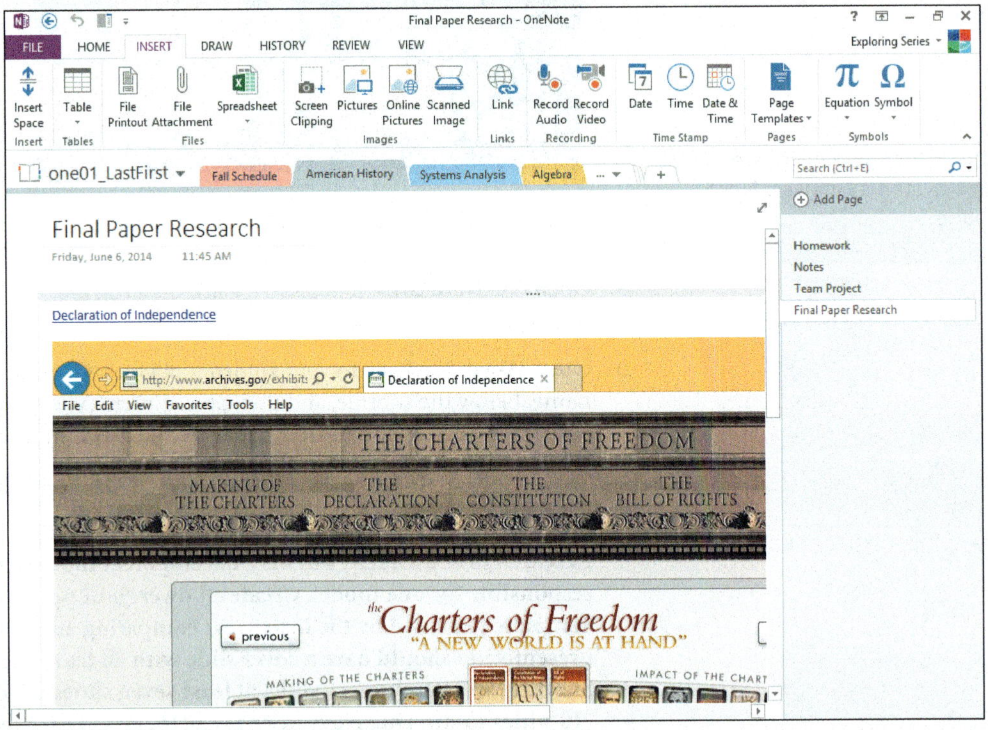

FIGURE 1.31 A screenshot of the www.archives.gov site is pasted into the American History Final Paper Research page.

a. Click the **American History Section tab**, and then click the **Final Paper Research Page tab**.

b. Click **Link** on the INSERT tab, in the Links group. Type **Declaration of Independence** in the Text to display text box. Type **http://www.ushistory.org/declaration/** in the Address text box. Click **OK** and then press **Enter**.

c. Maximize your browser, and navigate to **http://www.archives.gov/exhibits/charters /declaration.html** Click **Send to OneNote** in the taskbar. Click **Screen Clipping (S)**. Use the cross hairs to select the entire screen by clicking in the screen and dragging the mouse to select the contents of the screen. Select your **one01_LastFirst** notebook, in the Select Location in OneNote dialog box, and then select the **American History section**, expanding notebook and sections as needed. Select the **Final Paper Research page**, and then click **Send to Selected Location**. Close the browser.

d. Use the **Snipping Tool** to take a **Full-screen Snip**. Maximize Word. Click **Edit**. Click **Copy**. **Paste** the snip below the previous snip. Save and minimize Word. Close the Snipping Tool without saving.

STEP 3 » INSERT AND PASTE PHOTOS

Becky's instructor suggested she locate a picture of the signing of the Declaration of Independence to use in her final paper. After downloading the image to her storage media, she decided to paste it into her American History Final Paper Research page. Refer to Figures 1.32 and 1.33 as you complete Step 3.

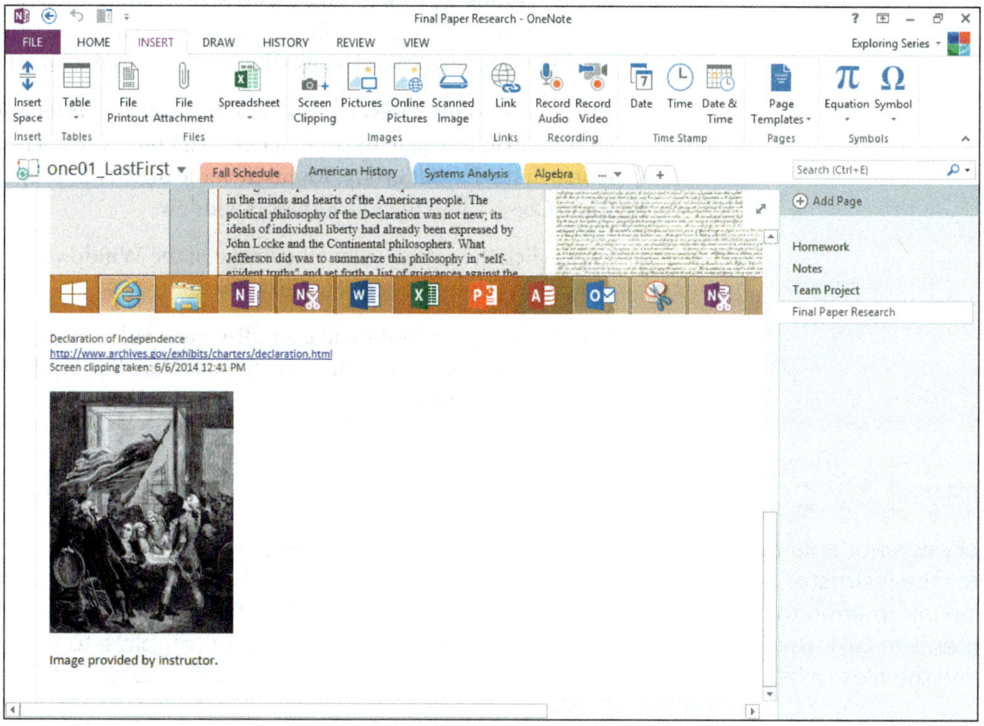

FIGURE 1.32 An image is inserted into the page.

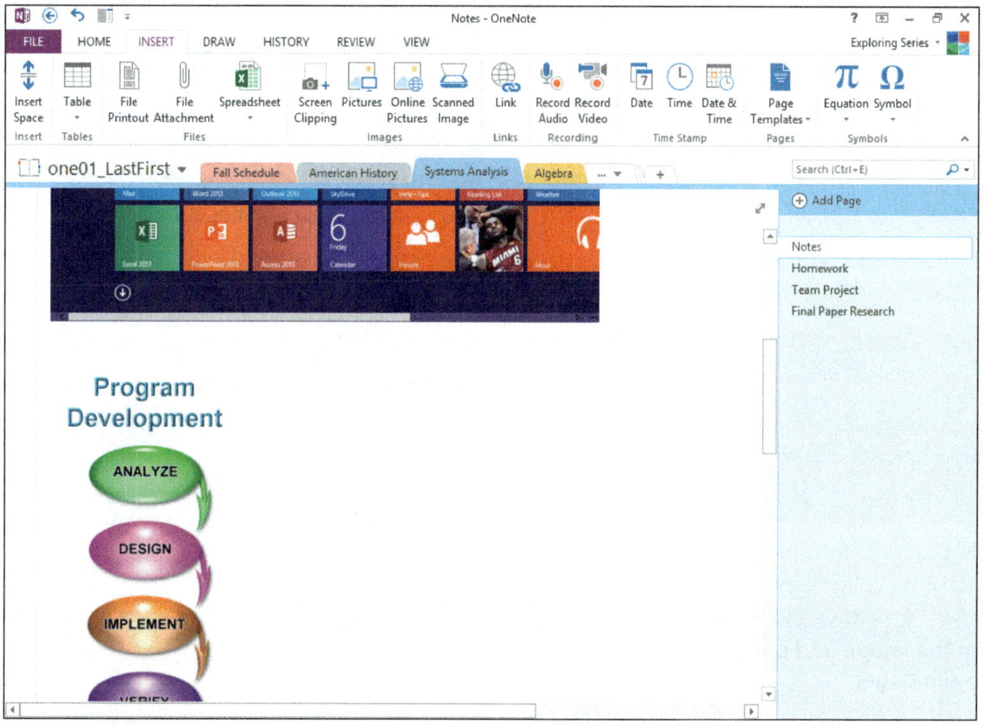

FIGURE 1.33 An image is copied and pasted into the page.

a. Click on **Final Paper Research page tab** in the American History section, if necessary. Click below the previously inserted information. Press **Enter**.

b. Click the **INSERT** tab, and then click **Pictures**, in the Images group. Navigate to the student data files. Select **one01h2_declaration.jpg**, and then click **Insert** and then press **Enter**.

c. Below the inserted image, type **Image provided by instructor.** Press **Enter**.

d. Use the **Snipping Tool** to take a **Full-screen snip**. Maximize Word. **Paste** the snip below the previous snip of research information on the American History Final Paper Research page. Save and minimize Word. Close the Snipping Tool without saving.

e. Click the **Systems Analysis section tab**. Click the **Notes page tab**. Click **File Explorer** in your taskbar. Navigate to your student data files. Click **View** in the Menu bar. Click **Large icons**, in the Layout group. Right-click the **one01h2_program_development.png** image. Click **Copy**. Close the File Explorer window.

f. Right-click the screen below the image of the Windows Start screen on the Notes page of the Systems Analysis section tab. Click **Paste**.

g. Use the **Snipping Tool** to take a **Full-screen snip**. Maximize Word. **Paste** the snip below the previous snip of the American History section. Save and minimize Word. Close the Snipping Tool without saving.

STEP 4 » CONVERT TEXT FROM AN IMAGE AND ATTACH A FILE

Becky was not able to attend the last Systems Analysis and Design Methods class. Her friend took a picture of the notes the instructor projected onto the whiteboard, and then sent her the image by e-mail. Becky would like to add some information to the notes. Because annotating the image is difficult, she has decided to convert the image contents to text. Becky's instructor sent a document and a PowerPoint template to the class. Becky would also like to attach the files to her notebook. Refer to Figures 1.34 through 1.36 as you complete Step 4.

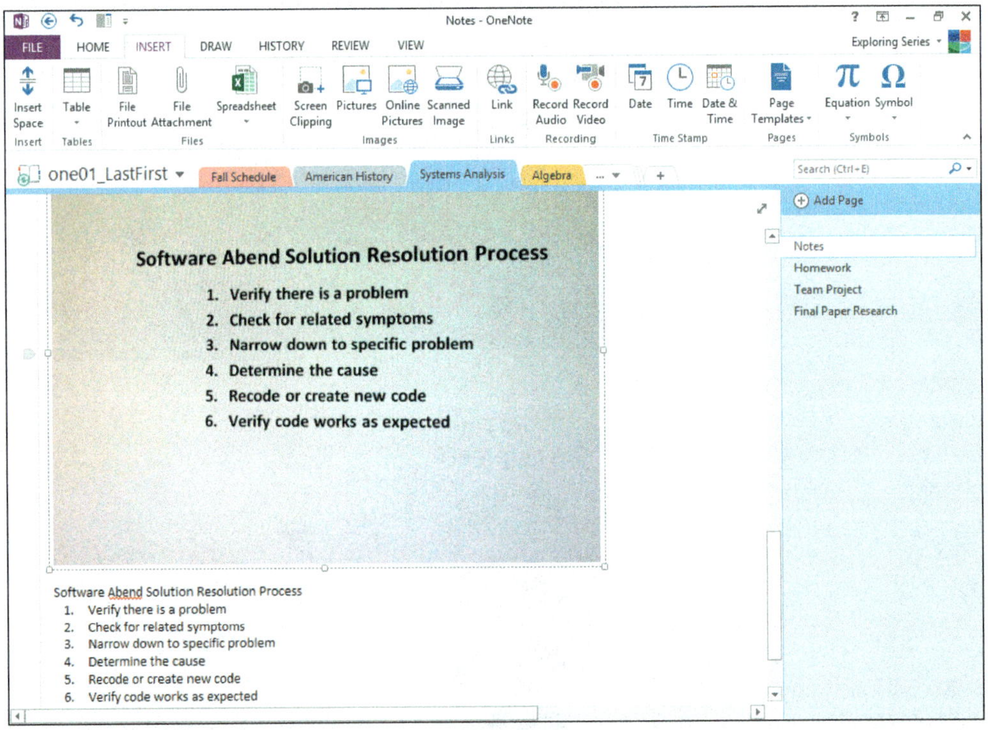

FIGURE 1.34 Text was copied from the image and pasted into the page.

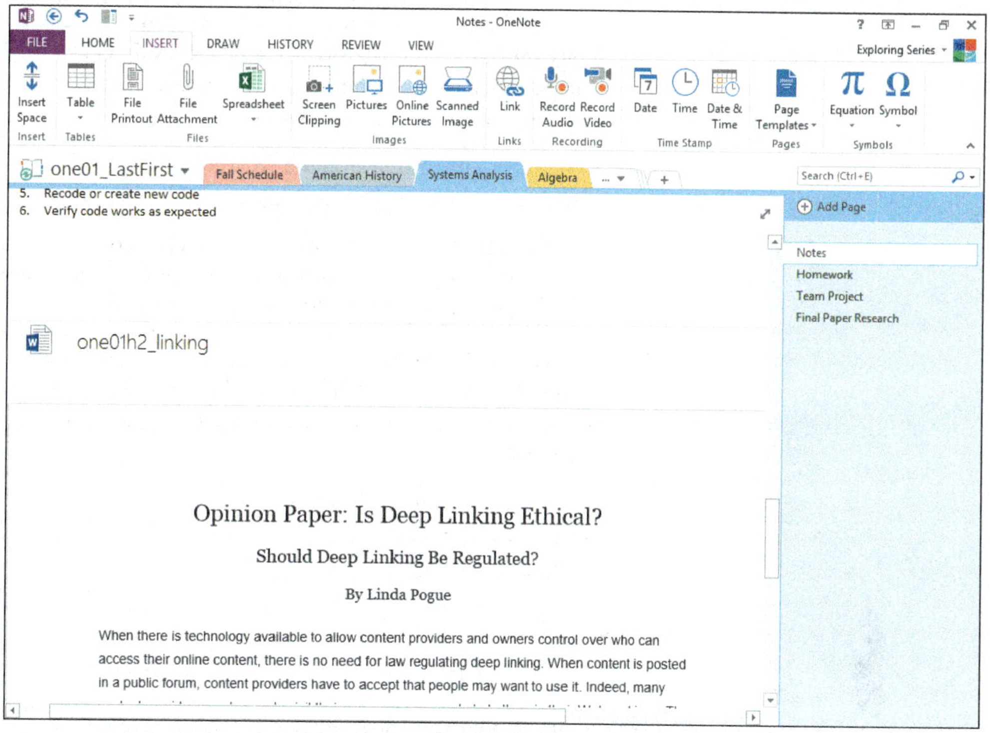

FIGURE 1.35 A printout of a file is inserted into the page.

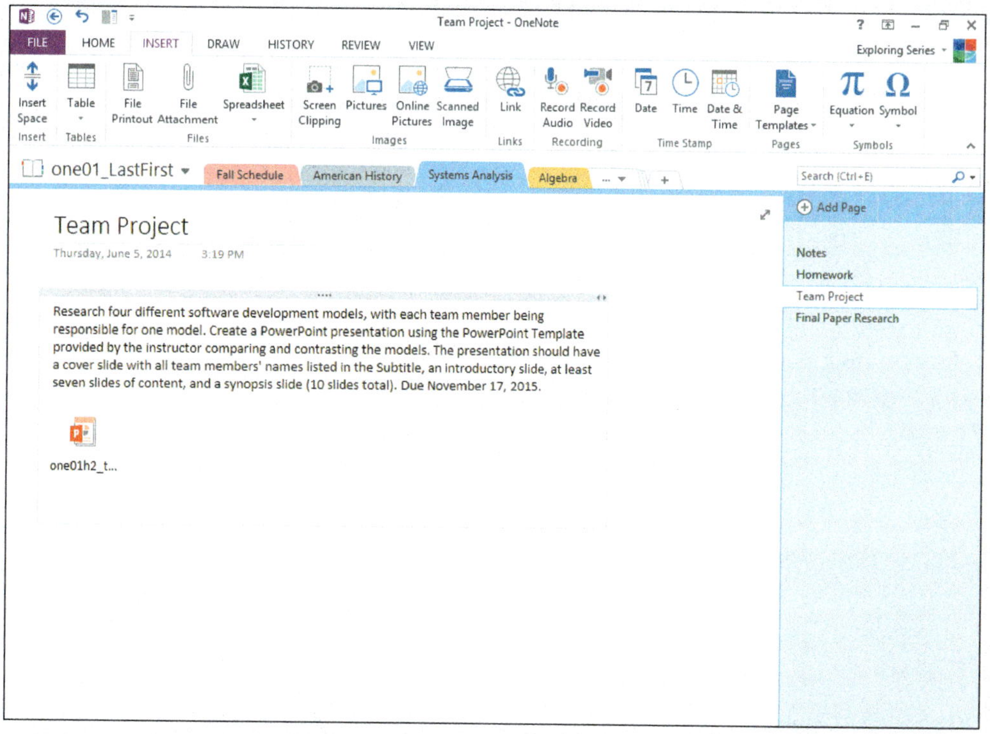

FIGURE 1.36 Assignment instructions are typed into the Systems Analysis Team Project page, and a PowerPoint template is attached to the page.

a. Click below the program development image, on the Systems Analysis Notes page. Click **Pictures**, on the INSERT tab, in the Images group. Navigate to your student data files. Select **one01h2_whiteboard.jpg**, and then click **Insert**.

b. Right-click the inserted image. Click **Copy Text from Picture**. Click below the image, and then click **Paste** on the HOME tab, in the Clipboard group. If necessary, make corrections to the pasted text to make it the same as the text in the image.

c. Use the **Snipping Tool** to take a **Full-screen snip**. Using the method previously practiced, copy the Snip. Maximize Word. **Paste** the snip below the snip of the program development image added to the Systems Analysis section Notes page. Save and minimize Word. Close the Snipping Tool without saving.

d. Click **File Attachment**, on the INSERT tab, in the Files group. Navigate to your student data files. Select the **one01h2_linking.docx** file, click **Insert**, and then click **Insert Printout**.

e. Use the **Snipping Tool** to take a **Full-screen snip**. Copy the snip. Maximize Word. **Paste** the snip below the previous snip of the program development image. Save and minimize Word. Close the Snipping Tool without saving.

f. Navigate to the **Systems Analysis section Team Project page**. Click below previously added content. Click the **INSERT tab**, and then click **File Attachment**, in the Files group. Navigate to your student data files. Select **one01h2_template.potx** and then click **Insert**. Click **Attach File**.

g. Use the **Snipping Tool** to take a **Full-screen snip**. Copy the snip. Maximize Word. **Paste** the snip below the previous snip. Save and minimize Word. Close the Snipping Tool without saving.

STEP 5 » CREATE A TABLE AND ADD A CALCULATION

Becky's Algebra homework requires her to use the formulas for the area of a circle, the Pythagorean theorem, and the Quadratic Equation. To help her remember these formulas, she will add them to her Algebra Notes page, and then use OneNote to calculate the area of a circle. Refer to Figure 1.37 as you complete Step 5.

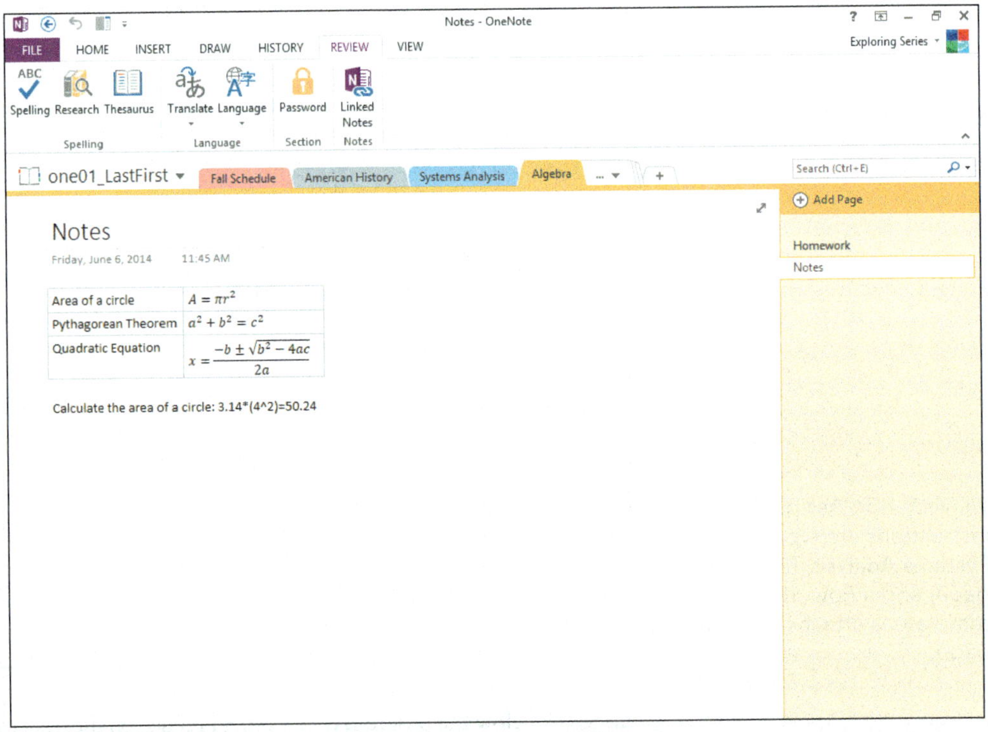

FIGURE 1.37 OneNote 2013 calculates the area of a circle.

a. Click below the date, on the **Algebra Notes page**, and then type **Area of a circle**. Press **Tab**. Click the **INSERT tab**, and then click the arrow below Equation, in the Symbols group. Click the box that displays the Area of Circle formula. Press **Enter**.

b. Type **Pythagorean Theorem** and then press **Tab**. Click the **INSERT tab**, and then click the arrow below Equation, in the Symbols group. Scroll to locate the Pythagorean Theorem. Click the box that displays the Pythagorean Theorem formula, then press **Enter**.

c. Type **Quadratic Equation** and then press **Tab**. Using the method above, locate the Quadratic Formula and then click the **box displaying the formula**. With the pointer on the right side table border, hold down the left mouse button and drag the border to the right until the formulas display.

> **TROUBLESHOOTING:** If the table does not expand when you drag the border, you have selected the container border instead of the table border.

d. Click in a blank area below the table. Type **Calculate the area of a circle: 3.14*(4^2)=** and then press the **Spacebar**. OneNote automatically calculates the value to be 50.24.

TIP Typing Equations with Exponents

When typing an equation that requires a number to be squared, cubed, or raised to the power of another number (an exponent), use the caret to indicate the number is raised to a power. On the standard QWERTY keyboard, the caret is the Shift+6 or ^.

e. Use the **Snipping Tool** to take a **Full-screen snip**. Maximize Word. **Paste** the snip below the previous snip. Save and close Word.

f. Submit the Word document to your instructor as directed.

STEP 6 » INTEGRATE OFFICE FILES

Becky's instructor e-mailed a document to review for homework and a spreadsheet that breaks down course grade points. After opening and reviewing the files, Becky has decided to add them to her notebook. Refer to Figures 1.38 and 1.39 as you complete Step 6.

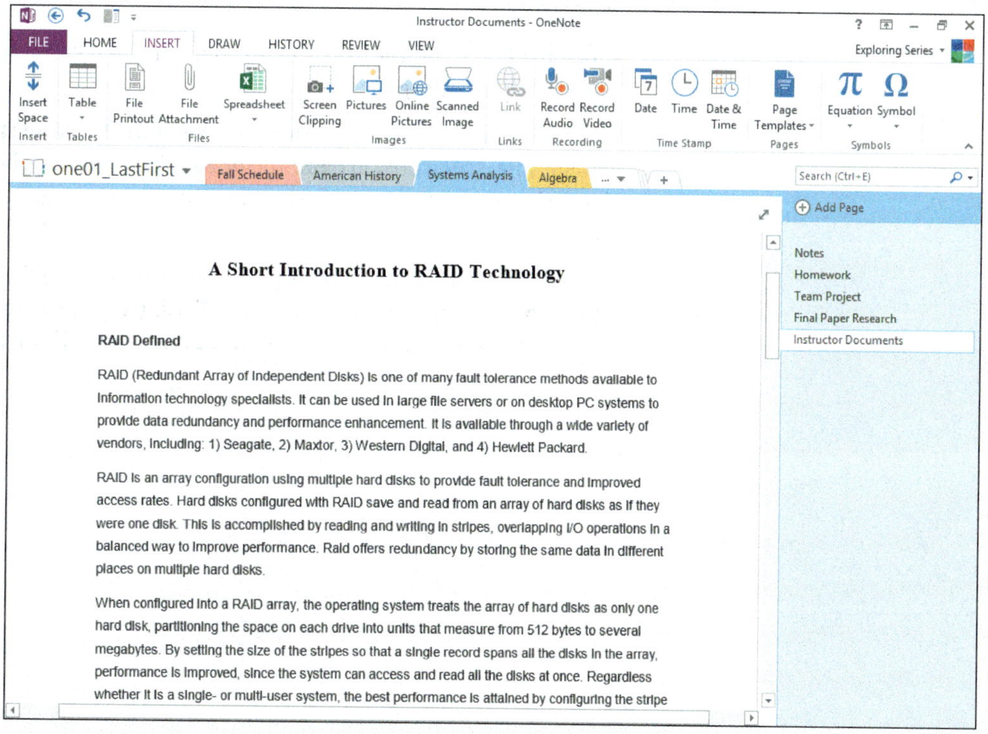

FIGURE 1.38 A Word file is sent to the Systems Analysis Instructor Documents page using Send to OneNote (D).

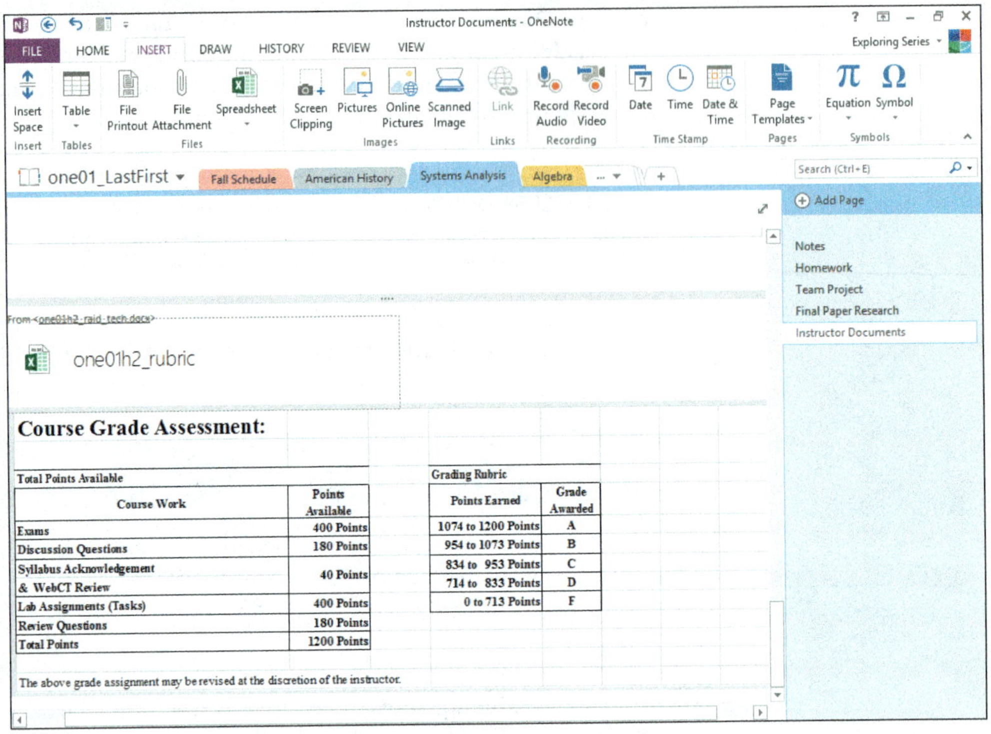

FIGURE 1.39 An Excel file is sent to the Systems Analysis Instructor Documents page using Send to OneNote (D).

a. Click the **Systems Analysis section**, add a page and title it **Instructor Documents**. Click on **File Explorer** on the taskbar. Navigate to your student data files. Open **one01h2_raid_tech.docx**. If necessary, click **Enable Editing**. Click **Send to OneNote** on the taskbar.

b. Click **Send to OneNote (D)** in the Send to OneNote window. **Expand** the appropriate notebook. **Expand** the Systems Analysis section. Select the **Instructor Documents** page, and then click **OK**. Close the document.

c. Use the **Snipping Tool** to take a **Full-screen snip**. Copy the snip. Maximize Word. **Paste** the snip below the previous snip. Save and minimize Word. Close the Snipping Tool without saving.

d. Open the **File Explorer**. Navigate to your student data files and open **one01h2_rubric.xlsx**. Click **Enable Editing**.

e. Click **Send to OneNote,** and then click **Send to OneNote (D)**, In the Select Location in OneNote dialog box, **expand** the **one01_LastFirst** notebook. **Expand** the **Systems Analysis** section. Select the **Instructor Documents page**, and then click **OK**. Click **Insert Spreadsheet**. Close Excel.

f. With the Instructor Documents page on the screen, use the **Snipping Tool** to take a **Full-screen snip**. Copy the snip. Maximize Word. **Paste** the snip below the previous snip of the inserted Word document. Save and minimize Word. Close the Snipping Tool without saving.

Chapter Objectives Review

After reading this chapter, you have accomplished the following objectives:

1. **Create and Manage Notebooks.**
   - Discovering the OneNote 2013 Interface - While similar to other Microsoft Office Applications, there are some differences in the OneNote ribbon. The interface includes the Quick Access Toolbar, the Ribbon, the Notebook Pane, Section tabs, Search bar, Page tabs, and the Page area.
   - Creating a Notebook and Adding Sections and Pages - Using Sections, you can customize a notebook to include all you need in one notebook, or create a notebook for each area of your life.
   - Deleting and Renaming Sections and Pages - As your needs change, you can add, rename, or delete sections and pages.
   - Copying or Moving a Notebook Section to Another Notebook - You can save time by copying or moving a notebook section to another notebook.
   - Rearranging Sections and Pages, and Merging Sections - After you have created a notebook, you may need to rearrange section or pages. You may find that some information spread through two or more sections needs to be in one section. Merging sections corrects this problem.
   - Saving, Printing, and Print Previewing a Notebook - OneNote automatically saves content added to it. In OneNote, you can only print a section or page. To print the entire notebook, you would have to print each section separately.
   - Send Notes using Outlook - Using Outlook, you can send sections of your notebook to a colleague or team member.
   - Export a Notebook - Since OneNote automatically saves to the location where the notebook was originally created, to make a backup or copy of the notebook, you must export the notebook.
2. **Add Content to OneNote.**
   - Adding Notes - OneNote provides containers for you to type into to add your notes. You can click anywhere in the page area to add a container.
   - Creating Screen Clips - You can use Windows key + PrtScn to create a screen clip, or use Send to OneNote (S) to capture part or all of a screen into a screenshot.
   - Capturing Internet Information - You can use Send to OneNote (S), Send to OneNote (D), or Windows key + PrtScn to capture Internet information.
   - Pasting or Inserting a Photo - To add images to your notebook, you can copy and paste an image on your screen, or insert a photo or other image file.
   - Inserting a Link - To insert a link, either copy and paste the URL from the address bar in your browser, or use the Link command in the Links group on the INSERT tab.
   - Converting Text from an Image - To capture text from an image, first insert or paste the image into your OneNote page, then right-click the image and click Copy Text from Picture. Click anywhere in the page area, and then paste the text into a new container.
   - Inserting a Scanned Image - With your image on the scanner, click the INSERT tab, click Scanned Image, select the appropriate device, set the resolution, then click Insert.
   - Attaching a File - To attach a file, click the INSERT tab, select the appropriate command from the Files, Images, or Recording groups, navigate to the file's location, and then click either Attach File, or Insert Printout.
   - Creating a Table - To create a table, type the contents of the first cell, then click Tab. Type the contents of the next cell, then use the Tab key to move to the next cell. When the row is complete, press Enter to move to the next row of the table.
   - Adding a Calculation - OneNote will calculate values for you. Type the equation using the math symbols *,/,-,+,^, and (). After the equation is typed, press the = key and then press the Spacebar.
   - Adding Audio or Video to a Page - With a microphone or webcam, you can record audio or video files in OneNote. To add existing audio or video files, use the File Attachment command in the Files group on the INSERT tab.
3. **Integrate Office Files.**
   - Inserting or Printing Files from Word, Excel, or PowerPoint - Use the INSERT tab, Files group commands to insert, attach, or print Microsoft Office files into OneNote.
   - Creating a New Spreadsheet - Create a new Excel spreadsheet from within OneNote using the Spreadsheet button in the Files group of the INSERT tab.
   - Using Send to OneNote - The Send to OneNote button, available on the taskbar when OneNote is open, allows you to send file contents from Word, Excel, and PowerPoint to a OneNote page

Key Terms Matching

For each question, locate the term that best completes the sentence. Write the letter of the correct term in the blank:

- **a.** Container
- **b.** Merge
- **c.** Notebook
- **d.** OneNote 2013
- **e.** Export
- **f.** Ribbon
- **g.** Page
- **h.** Optical Character Recognition (OCR)
- **i.** Path
- **j.** Quick Access Toolbar
- **k.** Screenshot
- **l.** Search bar
- **m.** Search scope
- **n.** Section
- **o.** Subpage
- **p.** Notebook Pane
- **q.** Snipping Tool
- **r.** Section tab
- **s.** Quick note
- **t.** Page pane

1. A(n) ______ is a file created by OneNote to hold content divided into sections and pages. **p. 2**
2. The ______ command is used to save a OneNote notebook package file to another location. **p. 9**
3. The ______ is a note that has not been placed into a specific page. **p. 21**
4. ______ is Microsoft's most recent note taking software for desktop computers. **p. 2**
5. A(n) ______ is an image created from the content displayed on your monitor. **p. 18**
6. The ______ allows you to find specific types of information in a notebook, section, or page. **p. 4**
7. A(n) ______ is the primary division in a notebook. **p. 2**
8. ______ software converts images to text. **p. 23**
9. The ______ contains four command buttons: Back, Undo, Dock to Desktop, and Customize. **p. 4**
10. A(n) ______ makes it possible to navigate from one notebook section to another. **p. 4**
11. A notebook page that is indented below a previous page is a(n) ______ **p. 6**
12. ______ is an accessory application that allows you to take a picture of your monitor screen. **p. 18**
13. The ______ is the exact route a computer uses to find a file. **p. 9**
14. A(n) ______ contains information inside a section. **p. 2**
15. ______ is the technique used to combine the contents of two or more pages, sections, or notebooks. **p. 8**
16. The ______ contains commands used to format content, insert content, draw illustrations, set passwords, or change the view of a notebook. **p. 4**
17. The ______ is the area of the OneNote screen that shows page tabs for all pages included in the current selected section. **p. 4**
18. The ______ allows users to easily navigate between open notebooks. **p. 4**
19. A(n) ______ is created when you click on the OneNote page, and is used to hold text, images, or other content. **p. 18**
20. The ______ determines where OneNote looks for information for which you are searching. **p. 4**

Multiple Choice

1. OneNote was first introduced in 2003 for:
   (a) MS-DOS
   (b) MacIntosh
   (c) Windows XP
   (d) DOS

2. Which of the following is NOT a way to add a new page to a section?
   (a) Right-click on an existing Page tab, and then click New Page
   (b) Right-click on an existing Sections tab, and then click New Page
   (c) Click the Add Page command at the top of the Page navigation pane
   (d) Press Ctrl+N

3. Which view removes all tabs from the screen?
   (a) Full Page View
   (b) Print Layout
   (c) Dock to Desktop
   (d) Normal View

4. When using the Windows key + PrtSc key to capture a screen clip, the image is automatically saved to the:
   (a) Snips folder
   (b) Screen capture folder
   (c) Screenshots folder
   (d) Image capture folder

5. The search ________ limits the pages, sections, or notebooks searched when searching for a specific term.
   (a) Scope
   (b) Bar
   (c) Explorer
   (d) Window

6. Common math functions can be added to your notebook by:
   (a) Clicking INSERT, and then clicking Insert Equation
   (b) Clicking REVIEW, and then clicking Add Equation
   (c) Clicking INSERT, and then clicking Equation
   (d) Clicking REVIEW, and then clicking Equation

7. Which of the following equations will be automatically calculated by OneNote?
   (a) 49/7+(32*39) equals
   (b) (4*35)+67=
   (c) =29+32*(63/9)
   (d) 39/3+42*16

8. To make a backup of a OneNote 2013 notebook, you would use the:
   (a) Copy command
   (b) Save As command
   (c) Print command
   (d) Export command

9. To easily navigate to another notebook, you would use the ________ Pane.
   (a) Page
   (b) Notebook
   (c) Section
   (d) Password

10. All deleted pages, sections, and notebooks are moved to the:
    (a) Deletions Folder
    (b) Notebook Recycle Bin
    (c) Notebook Deleted File Bin
    (d) Section Recycle Bin

Practice Exercises

1 Create a Notebook for a Blogger

Becky's cousin, Janetta, has been blogging on sewing topics for the past year. Janetta was excited at the possibility of using OneNote to manage her blogging activities and affiliate programs. She has asked you and Becky to help her create a OneNote notebook for her blogging activities.

a. Open Word. Open the *one01_p1_blogging* student data file. Click below the headers. If necessary, change the alignment to **Align Left**. Type **your name**, and then press **Enter**. Type the **current date**. Press **Enter** twice. Save the word file as **one01_p1_blogging_LastFirst**. Minimize Word.

b. Open OneNote 2013. Click the **FILE** tab, make sure **New** is selected, and then click your **OneDrive account**. Create a new notebook and name it **one01_p1_LastFirst**. If necessary, click **Not Now**. Name the New Section 1 section **Earnings**. Name the Untitled page **1st QTR**. Add a page and title it **2nd QTR**.

c. Add a new section and name it **Affiliate Programs**. Name the Untitled page **Approved Programs**. Add a new page and name it **Applied Programs**.

d. On the **Approved Programs page** in the Affiliate Programs section, type the following, pressing **Enter** after each line of text, except the last line:

   Amazon.com

   ShareASale

   Commission Junction

   Pepperjam

e. Using your choice of methods, capture a **full-screen screen shot**. Maximize Word. Paste the screen shot into the document below the date. Save and minimize Word.

f. Add a new section and name it **Blog**. Name the Untitled page **Future Articles**. Add a page and name it **Ideas for Articles**. Add a new section and name it **Schedule**. Name the Untitled page **Blog Schedule**.

g. Click the **Schedule** section tab and drag to move it before the **Earnings** section tab.

h. Using your choice of methods, capture a **full-screen screen shot**. Maximize Word. Paste the screen shot into the document below the first screen shot. Save and minimize Word.

i. On the **Blog Future Articles page** in the Blog section, click below the headings, click **INSERT** on the Ribbon, click **Pictures** in the Images group. Navigate to the student data files, select the data file named **one01_p1_sewing**, and then click **Insert**. Below the photograph, type **Photo by your name**, where *your name* is replaced by your own name, and then press **Enter**. Click **File Printout** in the Files group on the **INSERT** tab, navigate to the student data files, select **one01_p1_blog1** data file, and then click **Insert**. **Scroll** as necessary to display the lower half of the picture and the top paragraph of the article.

j. Using your choice of methods, capture a **full-screen screen shot**. Maximize Word. Paste the screen shot into the document below the second screen shot. Save and minimize Word. If used, close the Snipping Tool without saving.

k. Move the pointer below the one01_p1_blog1 data file printout. Type ********* and then press **Enter** (this is nine asterisks). Type **I need to take photos for the blog entries attached below**. Press **Enter**, click INSERT, click File Attachment in the Files group, navigate to your student data files and select the **one01_p1_blog2** data file. Click **Insert**, and then click **Attach File**. Use the same method to attach the **one01_p1_blog3** data file.

l. Using your choice of methods, capture a **full-screen screen shot**. Maximize Word. Paste the screen shot into the document below the printout of the blog entry. Save and minimize Word.

2 Add an Image, Convert an Image to Text, Add a Calculation and a Table

Janetta has asked for help adding content to the notebook. You will export the Practice 1 Exercise Notebook to create the Practice 2 Exercise Notebook.

a. Open Word. Open the *one01_p2_blogging* student data file. Click below the headers. If necessary, change the alignment to **Align Text Left**. Type **your name**, and then press **Enter**. Type the **current date**. Press **Enter** twice. Save the word file as **one01_p2_blogging_LastFirst**. Minimize Word.

b. Open OneNote 2013. If necessary, open **one01_p1_LastFirst**. Click the **FILE** tab, and then click **Export**. Select **Notebook** below Export Current, and then select **OneNote Package (*.onepkg)** below Select Format. Click **Export**. Navigate to your storage device, name the exported notebook **one01_p2_LastFirst**, and then click **Save**

c. Navigate to your storage device, and double-click **one01_p2_LastFirst**. In the Unpack Notebook dialog box, click **Create**.

d. Add a page to the **Blog** section and name it **Sewing Tips** and press **Enter**. If necessary, click **INSERT** on the ribbon, click **Pictures** in the Images group, navigate to your student data files and select **one01_p2_convert**. Click **Insert**. Right-click the image, and then click **Copy Text from Picture**. Move the pointer below the image and click **Paste** in the Clipboard group on the **Home** tab.

e. Click the **REVIEW** tab on the ribbon. Click **Spelling** in the Spelling group. Accept the corrections recommended by the Spelling Checker. In the dialog box that states the spelling check is complete, click **OK**.

f. Click below the text copied from the picture. Type **36*2.54=** and then press the **space bar**. The solution, 91.44, will automatically be calculated.

g. Using your choice of methods, capture a **full-screen screen shot**. Maximize Word. Paste the screen shot into the document below the date. Save and minimize Word. Close the Snipping Tool without saving.

h. Add a page to the Blog section and name it **Blogs to Follow** and press **Enter**. Use your browser to search for **sewing blogs**. Click on one blog from the results to open the web site. Maximize the browser screen. Click **Send to OneNote**, and then click **Screen Clipping (S)**. Click in the top left corner of the monitor screen. Hold the left mouse button and drag to the bottom right corner to select the entire screen. **Expand** the one01_p2_LastFirst notebook in the Select Location in OneNote dialog box. **Expand** the Blog section. Click **Blogs to Follow**, and then click **Send to Selected Location**.

i. In the browser, navigate to your search results. Select and open a different blog. Use **Windows Key + PrtScn** to capture a screen print. In OneNote, on the Blogs to Follow page, click below the screen clipping and then use **Ctrl + V** to paste the second blog screen clipping onto the page.

j. Using your choice of methods, capture a **full-screen screen shot**. Maximize Word. Paste the screen shot into the document below the previous snip. Save and minimize Word.

k. Click the **1st QTR** page tab in the Earnings section. Click on the 1st QTR page, click on the **INSERT** tab, and then click **Spreadsheet** in the Files group, and then click **Existing Excel Spreadsheet**. Navigate to your student data files, select **one01_p2_earnings**, click **Insert**, and then click **Insert Spreadsheet**.

l. With the 1st QTR page active, click **File**. Click **Print**, and then click **Print Preview**. Use the following settings: **Current Page**, **Letter paper size**, **Scale content to paper width**, and **Portrait**. In the Footer, select **Page (number)**.

m. Using your choice of methods, capture a **full-screen screen shot**. Maximize Word. Paste the screen shot into the document below the previous snip. Save and minimize Word. Close the Print Preview and Settings dialog box.

n. Click the **Applied Programs** page tab in the Affiliate Programs section. Below the page date, type the following, using the **Tab** and **Enter** keys as needed to create the table:

Affiliate Program Application	URL	Date Applied
Juniper Online Sales	Juniperonlinesales.com	June 15, 2016
Make Sales Now	Makesalesnow.com	June 28, 2016
Infinity Online Sales	Infinityonlinesales.com	August 12, 2016

o. Using your choice of methods, capture a **full-screen screen shot**. Maximize Word. Paste the screen shot into the document below the previous snip. Save and minimize Word.

p. Click **FILE**. Click **Share**. Click **Invite People**. Type **your instructor's e-mail address** in the To text box. In the message, type **My notebook is one01_p2_LastFirst.**

> **TROUBLESHOOTING:** If you get a message that you need to put the notebook on OneDrive to share it, you did not save the notebook to your OneDrive account in step b. On the Share screen, click Move Notebook to move the notebook to OneDrive.

q. Capture a **full-screen screen shot**. In OneNote, press **Share**. Maximize Word. **Paste** the screen shot into the document below the previous snip. Save and close Word. If necessary, close the Snipping Tool without saving. Close OneNote 2013. Submit the Word document as directed by your instructor.

> **NOTE:** After the notebook is shared, you will see vertical lines beside content with your initials next to them. This is normal. You will learn about this in Chapter 2.

Mid-Level Exercises

1 Create a Notebook for a Culinary Student

Your neighbor, Jason Belton, dreams of becoming a chef and opening his own bistro. He is attending a culinary school, and has asked you to help him set up a notebook to keep up with his classes.

a. Open Word. Open the *one01_m1_culinary* data file. If necessary, click **Enable Editing**. Click below the headers. If necessary, change the alignment to **Align Text Left**, type **your name** on the first line, press **Enter**, and then type the **current date**. Press **Enter** twice. Save the Word document as **one01_m1_culinary_LastFirst** and then minimize the document.

b. Create a notebook using your desktop OneNote 2013 application. Name the notebook **one01_m1_ LastFirst**. If necessary, click **Not Now**. Name the untitled section **School**.

c. In the School section, create four pages titled **Food Science**, **Pastry Techniques**, **Assignments**, and **Gastronomy**. Right-click the **Food Science** page, add a page named **Project**. Right-click the **Project** page tab, and then click **Make Subpage**. Using the same method, on the **Gastronomy** page, add a subpage named **Research**.

d. Using your choice of methods, capture a **full-screen screen shot**. Maximize Word. Paste the screen shot into the document below the date. Save and minimize Word.

e. Create three pages named **Notes**, **Recipes**, and **Equipment Needed**. Drag these three pages up below the Pastry Techniques page, and then make all three pages into **subpages**. Drag the **Equipment Needed** subpage tab up until it is directly below the Notes subpage.

f. On the Recipes subpage, from the INSERT tab, use **File Printout** to insert the **one01_m1_recipe1** student data file.

g. Using your choice of methods, capture a **full-screen screen shot**. Maximize Word. Paste the screen shot into the document below the first screen shot. Save and minimize Word.

h. On the Pastry Techniques Notes subpage, use the same method used in Step f to print the **one01_ m1_ handout** student data file to the page.

i. Using your choice of methods, capture a **full-screen screen shot**. Maximize Word. Paste the screen shot into the document below the second screen shot. Save and minimize Word.

j. On the Pastry Techniques Equipment Needed sub-page, type **Supplies needed for this semester:** Press **Enter** twice, type **Item**, and then press **Tab**. Type **Cost** and then press **Enter**. Type **Deluxe cake decorating tip set**, and then press **Tab**. Type **$29.99**, and then press **Enter**. Type **2 pastry bags**, and then press **Tab**. Type **$13.90**, and then press **Enter**. Type **Pastry blender**, and then press **Tab**. Type **$9.77**, and then press **Enter**. Type **Cake spatula set**, and then press **Tab**. Type **$35.97**.

k. Select the four items beneath the Item heading, and then on the HOME tab, add a **To Do Tag** to them.

   As the items are purchased, they can be checked off the list.

l. Click below the table and then type **$29.99+13.90+9.77+35.97=** and then press the **space bar**.

   The total will be $89.63.

m. Using your choice of methods, capture a **full-screen screen shot**. Maximize Word. Paste the screen shot into the document below the third screen shot. Save and minimize Word.

n. Add a sub-page to the Recipes page and title the sub-page **Cookie Recipes**. Insert the **one01_m1_ recipe2** student data file image. Right-click the image, and copy the text from the image. Paste it to the page below the image. Make any needed corrections to the pasted text. Note that the ingredients will be in a single column.

o. Using your choice of methods, capture a **full-screen screen shot**. Maximize Word. Paste the screen shot into the document below the fourth screen shot. Save and close Word.

p. Submit the Word document as directed by your instructor.

2 Use Send to OneNote and Insert a Spreadsheet

Jason has asked you to demonstrate how to add more content to the notebook.

a. Open Word. Open the *one01_m2_culinary* data file. If necessary, click **Enable Editing**. Click below the headers. If necessary, change the alignment to **Align Text Left**, type **your name** on the first line, press **Enter**, and then type the **current date**. Press **Enter** twice. Save the Word document as **one01_m2_culinary_LastFirst** and then minimize the document.

b. In OneNote, open the **one01_m1_LastFirst** notebook. Click the FILE tab, and then click Export. Export the Notebook to your storage media, using the name **one01_m2_LastFirst**.

c. Unpack the one01_m2_LastFirst notebook.

d. Right-click the **Recipes** subpage and add a new subpage titled **Pie Recipes**. Move the **Pie Recipes** page up below the Cookie Recipes sub-page.

e. In your browser, navigate to **www.cooks.com/recipe/g04k506s/lemon-pie.html**. Scroll to display the entire recipe on the screen. Use **Send to OneNote Screen Clipping (S)** to send the recipe to your **Pie Recipes** sub-page.

f. Using your choice of methods, capture a **full-screen screen shot**. Maximize Word. Paste the screen shot into the document below the date. Save and minimize Word.

g. Delete the **Food Science** page tab. Delete the **Project** page tab.

   Jason has decided to work part-time this semester, and dropped Food Science due to a scheduling conflict.

h. In your browser, navigate to **www.allrecipes.com/recipe/perfect-pumpkin-pie/**. Right-click the photo, and then click Copy (in Firefox, click Copy Image; in Google Chrome, click Copy Image). On the **Pie Recipes** sub-page, click below the pie recipe, and then paste the image. Paste the **URL of the page** the image was taken from below the image.

i. In your browser, scroll until the pumpkin pie recipe is on the screen. Use **Send to OneNote Screen Clipping (S)** to take a **full screen clip**. Send the screen clip to the **Pie Recipes** subpage.

j. In OneNote, scroll until the bottom half of the pie image displays at the top of the screen.

k. Using your choice of methods, capture a **full-screen screen shot**. Maximize Word. Paste the screen shot into the document below the recipe screen shot. Save and minimize Word.

l. Click the **Assignments** page tab. On the **INSERT** tab, click Spreadsheet, and then click **Existing Excel Spreadsheet**. Navigate to your student data files, and insert the **one01_m2_courses** file on your Assignments page. Rename the page **Courses**.

m. Using your choice of methods, capture a **full-screen screen shot**. Maximize Word. **Paste** the screen shot into the document below the pumpkin pie screen shot. Save and minimize Word.

n. Prepare to send the **Equipment Needed** page to your instructor by e-mail. Do not press Send. Capture a **full-screen screen shot**. Maximize Word. Paste the screen shot into the document below the courses screen shot. Close the Outlook window without sending or saving the e-mail.

o. Click the **FILE tab**, and then click **Export**. Export the Notebook to your storage media, using the name **one01_m2_LastFirst**.

p. Save and close Word. Close the e-mail window without sending. Close OneNote.

q. Submit the Word document as directed by your instructor.

Beyond the Classroom

General Case

Create a PowerPoint presentation for incoming freshmen on ways nonprofit companies could use OneNote to keep stakeholders and volunteers informed of key information:

- Name the presentation **one01_gc_OneNote_LastFirst**.
- A cover slide with an appropriate title and your name in the subtitle.
- An introductory slide that explains what the presentation will cover.
- A minimum of four slides of content.
- At least two appropriate images of your choice (these can be screenshots).
- A summary slide.
- A works cited slide with all images, including screenshots.

Submit the presentation as directed by your instructor.

Research Case

In preparation for graduation, use the Internet to research at least five companies for whom you are interested in working, based on your field of study. Use the skills you learned in this chapter to create a job search OneNote notebook and name it **one01_rc_Jobs_LastFirst**. For each company you research, create a section. In each section, include pages for company history and facts, information concerning the procedure for applying, and the types of positions available. The notebook should also have at least two subpages. Select at least one position and use the Internet to research salary ranges for that position in your area. Record your findings on a page in the notebook. Share your notebook with your instructor.

Disaster Recovery

While working with the blogging notebook you and Becky created for her, Janetta accidentally deleted the Earnings Section tab. Janetta called you for help in retrieving the deleted section. Create a new Word document and save it as **one01_dr_LastFirst**. Type your name and the current date on the first two lines at the top of the page. Using a numbered list, write step-by-step instructions explaining how to find the deleted section in the Recycle Bin and retrieve it. Save the document and submit it as directed by your instructor.

Capstone Exercise

Programming Team Notebook

As a student intern for Search It, Inc., you have been asked to create a OneNote notebook for the Server Side Programming Team. The notebook will contain sections and pages to provide information and announcements to the team.

This assignment will be submitted by sharing the notebook with your instructor.

a. Create a notebook named **one01_capstone_LastFirst** and save it to your OneDrive account. Click **Not Now**.

b. Create four sections titled **Activities, Notes, Contacts,** and **Announcements.**

c. In the Announcements section, name the Untitled page **Team Announcements**. On the page, attach the **one01_c_evaluation** data file and then press **Enter**. Insert a printout of the **one01_c_team_announcements** data file.

d. **Add a subpage** below the Team Announcements page titled **Company Stationery** and then press **Enter** twice. Type **As of August 1, 2016, all written correspondence to vendors and suppliers must be typed on company letterhead stationery. The letterhead template is attached below**. Press **Enter** twice. Attach the **one01_c_letterhead_template** data file.

e. In the **Activities** section, name the Untitled page **Company Activities**, and then insert a file printout of the *one01_c_picnic* data file.

f. Open the *one01_c_addresses* data file in Word 2013. If necessary, Enable Editing. **Select** and **copy** all contents. In OneNote, navigate to the **Contacts** section. Name the Untitled page **Team Contacts**, and then press **Enter**. **Paste** the team addresses. Add a **blank line** above Carla Gardner's name. On the blank line, type the following, pressing **Enter** after each line:

Your name

1111 W. Somewhere Dr.

Liberty Mountain, TX 78642

(555) 555-1234

FirstInitialLastName@searchit.com

Press **Enter**.

g. Move the section tabs until they are in this order:

Activities, Announcements, Contacts, Notes.

h. Your team will be learning HTML and JavaScript to build a vendor's access web page. Name the Untitled page in the Notes section **HTML Notes.**

i. In your browser, navigate to **http://www.w3schools.com/html/**. In the left menu bar, click **HTML Introduction.** Using **Send to OneNote Screen Clipping (S)** to send a **screen clip** of the code in the HTML Example box, starting with *HTML Example* and ending with *<html>*, to the HTML Notes page.

j. Right-click the image (screen clipping), click **Copy Text from Picture.** Paste the text below the image. Make corrections to the pasted text, so that the text matches that in the image.

k. Add a subpage to the Team Announcements page titled **Team Shirts** below the Company Stationery subpage, and press Enter. Type **Team Shirt with Logo** and **Bold** the text. Press **Enter** twice. Insert the **one01_c_team_logo** data file as an attachment. Press **Enter** twice. Type **Carla and Abe have finished the team logo for our team shirts**. Press **Enter** twice.

l. Type the following, pressing **Tab** after the first two column entries and **Enter** after the third column entry:

T-Shirt Color	Sizes	Price
White	S, M, L, XL	$15.99
White	XXL, XXXL	$18.99
Black	S, M, L, XL	$15.99
Black	XXL, XXXL	$18.99

m. Below the table, type **Be sure to add 8.5% tax to your order. To figure the total due on your order, multiply the shirt subtotal by 1.085**. Press **Enter**.

n. Type **Example: (2*$18.99)*1.085=** and then press the **Space Bar**.

The calculation total is $41.2083. OneNote may round this total to $41.21. If not, team members will round this amount to $41.21 when they pay for the shirts.

o. In the Notes section, add a subpage titled **Adding Video** to the HTML Notes page. Press **Enter**.

p. Research **HTML add video**. Find a web site with the appropriate information, and use **Send to OneNote Screen Clipping (S)** to select the **first full screen of information from the two web pages** and send them to the Notes section **Adding Video** subpage.

q. Add a subpage to the HTML Notes page titled **Adding Audio**, and then press **Enter**. Find two more websites with information on adding audio. **Copy** and **paste** the URLs for these two web sites below the *Adding Audio* heading.

r. **Check spelling** on all sections, making any necessary corrections.

s. **Share** the **one01_capstone_LastFirst** notebook with **your instructor**. If necessary, log into your OneDrive account to complete the share. Export the one01_capstone_LastFirst notebook to your storage media. It will be used in the Chapter 2 Capstone.

t. Close OneNote 2013. **Log out** of OneDrive.

OneNote 2013

Formatting and Collaborating Online with OneNote

CHAPTER 2

Tools, Templates, and Collaboration with OneNote Notebooks and the OneNote App

berc/fotolia

OBJECTIVES

AFTER YOU READ THIS CHAPTER, YOU WILL BE ABLE TO:

CASE STUDY | Student Intern

Bonnie Duckett's new OneNote 2013 skills have landed her a student intern position with Search It, an online search engine company. As an undergraduate student majoring in Information Systems Management in the College of Technology & Computing at Pearson University, Bonnie uses OneNote to help track her courses. She develops OneNote notebooks for others, too. In her internship, she creates OneNote notebooks for her team and for her manager.

Use Tools and Templates

OneNote provides many tools to help you organize and format your notes and pages. In this section, you will learn about formatting text, applying a template, and using pen and drawing tools. In addition, you will learn how to spell check your notes, use the built-in thesaurus to find just the right word, add tags to notes, and password protect a section.

Use Text Formatting Tools

STEP 1 ›› Formatting text using color, size, weight, and style can add interest and emphasis. For instance, using bold, red text to indicate information that may be on a final exam would help it be more memorable, and easier to locate on the page. Too much formatting can be a hindrance, though. If all text is red and bold, finding specific information to study for an exam will be difficult. Some colors such as yellow or cyan are difficult to read, especially if there are long paragraphs of the text formatted with these colors.

When formatting text, keep in mind the reason you are formatting it. Use bold, italics, and color in a consistent manner. Basic black text on a white screen is the most easily read combination, but using some color can be helpful in locating specific information in your notes or in memorizing content.

To add formatting to text, click the HOME tab. In the Basic Text group, select the appropriate commands for the font, font size, font color, and font style such as bold or italic. Highlighting text, using bullet points, and headings also make information on the page more memorable. Tags will be covered in a later section.

To copy the text formatting from one section or area to another, select the text with the correct formatting, click ***Format Painter*** in the Clipboard group of the HOME tab, then drag the Format Painter pointer over the text you need to change. After you release the left mouse button, the Format Painter automatically turns off. If you are making multiple changes, for instance changing all the page titles in all pages of all sections, you can format the title on one page, select the text, double-click Format Painter, and then navigate to each page and drag the pointer over the title to make the format changes. After you complete making the formatting changes, click Format Painter again to turn it off. A single click enables you to copy the format to another area once, whereas double-clicking the Format Painter toggles it on, and it will remain on until you click the button again.

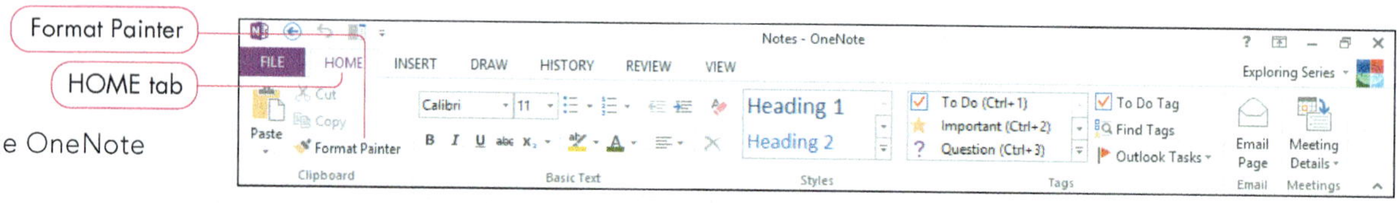

FIGURE 2.1 The OneNote HOME tab.

Apply a Page Template

In OneNote, ***page templates*** are used to add predesigned page designs and formats. Using page templates saves time in creating pages, and adds consistency to the overall notebook design. Page templates are available in the Pages group on the INSERT tab. There are Academic, Blank, Business, Decorative, and Planners templates installed with OneNote. In addition, you can go online to find templates on Office.com. To use a template:

1. Select the appropriate section and page.
2. On the INSERT tab, in the Pages group, click the top half of the Page Templates button.
3. Click the major heading desired, such as Academic.
4. Click on the specific template. Some templates will have background colors and images, whereas others will be simple or blank.

For a notebook that contains sections for each class, you might add a Simple Lecture Notes page template from the Academic templates to each course section. This page template provides a preformatted page with places for homework and notes. If you do not find the page template you need, you can click Templates on Office.com to search through Microsoft's available template styles.

Page colors can also be changed using a template in the Blank heading. If page colors are changed, you may also want to change the Section tab to match the color. To change the color of a Section tab, right-click on the tab, point to Section Color, and then select the desired color from the list.

Create a Page Template

If you need a template that is not available in the template gallery, you can create your own template. To create a template, use the following steps:

1. Click on the Page tab where you want to create the template.
2. Add text, images, or other content.
3. Format text as desired.
4. On the INSERT tab, in the Pages group, click the top half of the Page Templates command.
5. At the bottom of the Templates pane, click Save current page as a template.
6. Click Save.

OneNote will create a new template heading titled My Templates in the ***template gallery***. The template you created will be located within My Templates, a template heading. To use your page template, use the same method as applying any other page template.

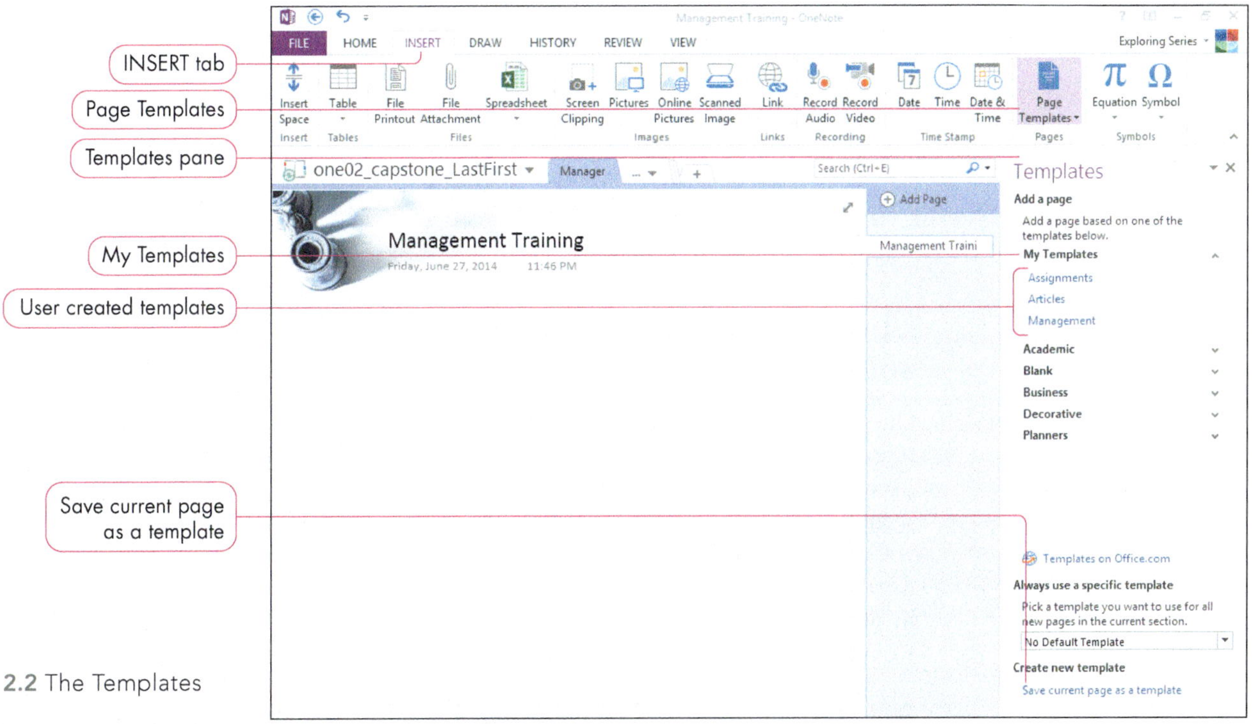

FIGURE 2.2 The Templates pane.

Use Pen and Drawing Tools

In OneNote, the pen and drawing tools are primarily designed for use with a tablet and either your finger or a stylus. Whereas it is possible to use these features with a mouse, the results may not be suitable for notetaking. For example, writing class notes in the page area with a mouse is difficult, and requires more practice than most people are willing to put into it. Notes written into the page area can be changed to typed text using the following steps:

1. Click the DRAW tab.
2. Select your choice of Pen tools.
3. Use a mouse, mouse pen, finger, or stylus to write a note on the notebook page.
4. Click Lasso Select.
5. Select the written note using your mouse to outline it. In the Convert group, click Ink to Text.

The conversion to text may not be exact, so you may have to click into the container holding the text and make corrections. The pen and drawing tools can also be used for creating mind maps, sketches, or drawings that illustrate your typed notes.

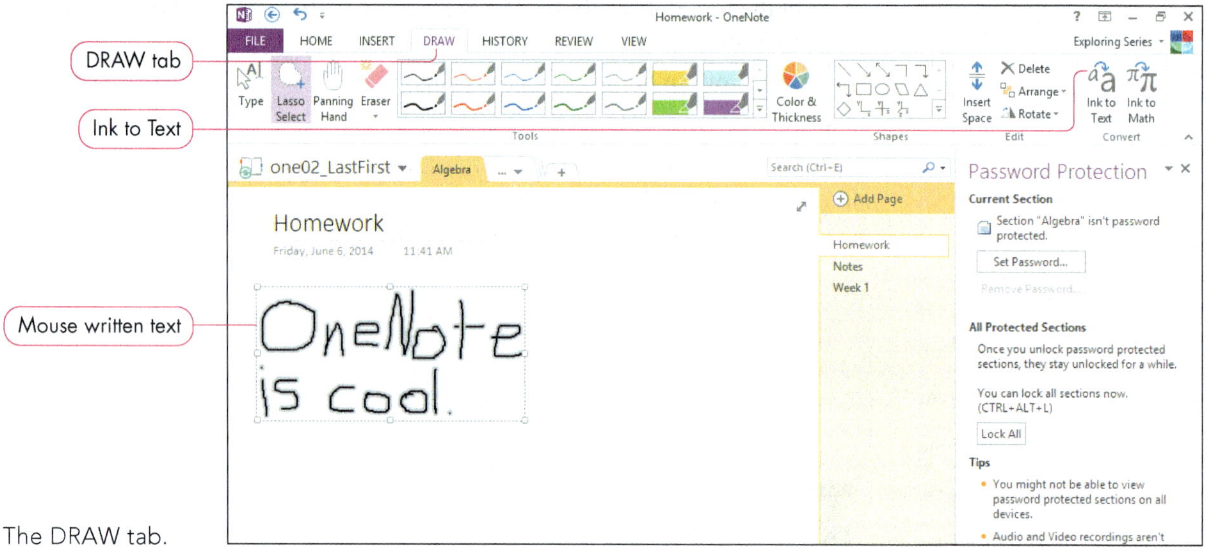

FIGURE 2.3 The DRAW tab.

Check Spelling, Use a Thesaurus, and Research a Topic

STEP 2» OneNote will check your spelling, but it can only check against the built-in dictionary. If you type a real word used incorrectly, it may not catch it. For this reason, you should always read over your notes, even after you check spelling. For example, if you typed: "Dud ewe sea eye scent to limbs two yore form?" when you intended to type "Did you see I sent two lambs to your farm?", OneNote would find nothing wrong with the sentence. This is because all the words are in the dictionary, even though they have been misused. The Spelling Checker is a helpful tool, but should not be trusted to catch all your mistakes. To check spelling, click the REVIEW tab, and then click Spelling.

The REVIEW tab also provides access to research a topic or locate a synonym using the thesaurus. Suppose you are taking a programming class and must use the quadratic equation in a program that will solve math problems when you input variables, but you do not remember the quadratic equation formula. On the REVIEW tab, in the Spelling group, click Research. In the Research pane, type in *quadratic equation*. OneNote uses Bing to search the Internet and returns results that may be what you need. Click on the link below the search results you are interested in reviewing, and your default web browser will open to display the

Web site. You can easily use the Send to OneNote button to take a screen clipping that gives the basic information about the quadratic equation and provides the formula. This sends a clipping of the Web site to your active OneNote page.

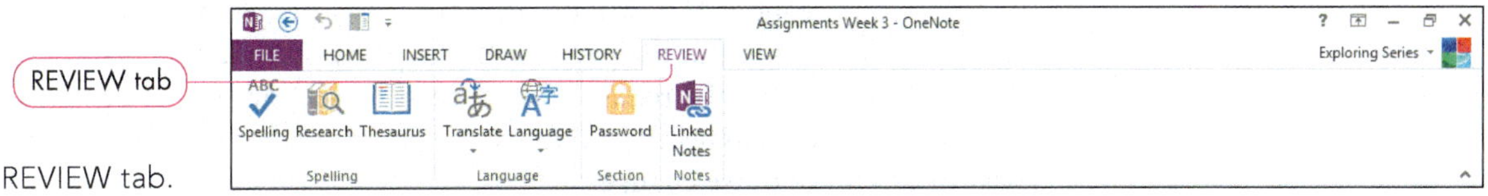

FIGURE 2.4 The REVIEW tab.

Apply a Password

STEP 3

In OneNote, you can password protect individual sections of a notebook. This feature should be used with care. If you forget the password, you cannot retrieve the password, and will never be able to access your information. If you are using OneNote on your own computer, and will not have others using your computer, password protection may not interest you. However, if you share your notebook with someone else, ***password protection*** prevents them accessing sensitive information. Password protection can be added to a section in your desktop application, but at the time of this writing, this option was not available in the OneNote Web App.

To apply password protection:

1. Make sure the section you want to password protect is the current active section.
2. On the REVIEW tab, in the Section group, click Password.
3. In the Password Protection pane, click Set Password.
4. In the Password Protection dialog box, type your password in the Enter Password text box.
5. Retype it in the Confirm Password text box.
6. Click OK.

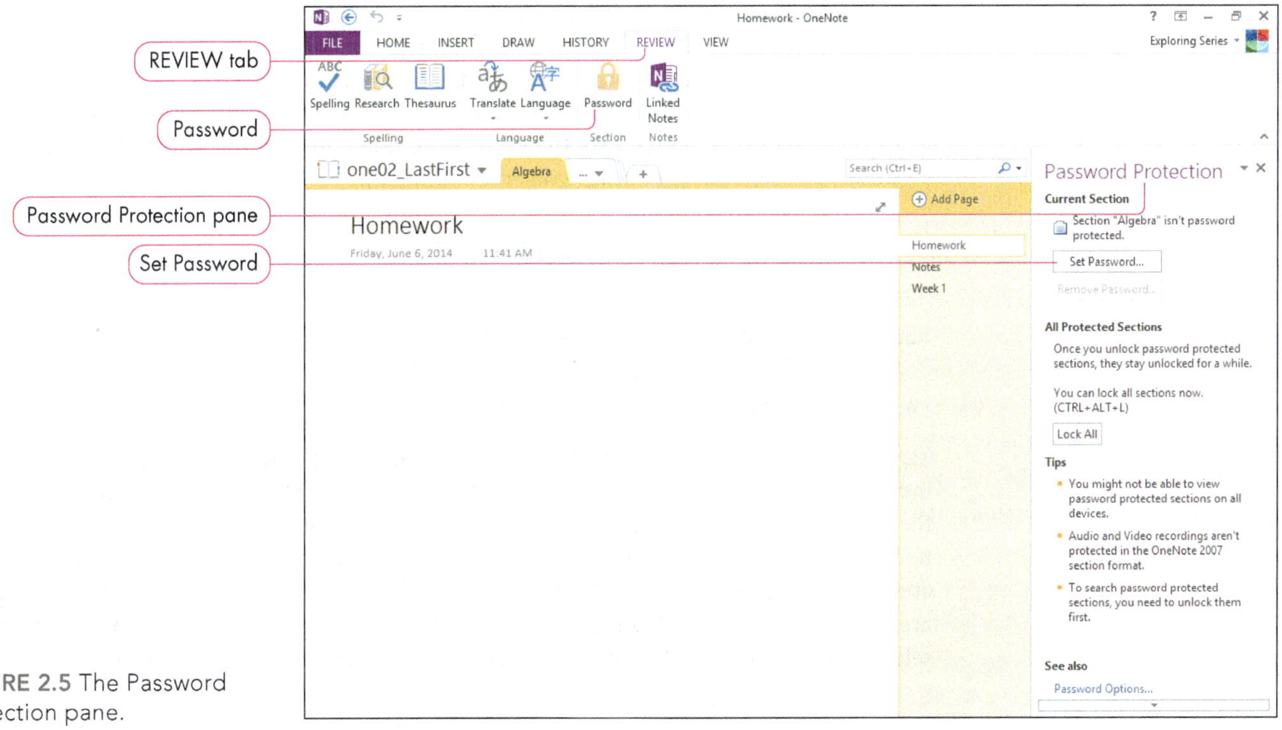

FIGURE 2.5 The Password Protection pane.

If the passwords match, OneNote will enable you to click OK. If not, you will be required to re-enter them. Again, if you lose or forget the password, you will not be able to recover your notes.

For security sake, do not put the password on a sticky note and stick it to your monitor or under your keyboard. It sounds silly, but many people do just that. If you must write it down to remember it, put the paper with the password in a safe place. Once the password is set, you must provide the password to access the section. In the Password Protection pane, you can change the password or remove the password, but you will need to know the current password to make those changes.

Once password protected sections are unlocked, they stay unlocked for a period of time, and will automatically relock when OneNote is closed. To relock the section or sections without closing OneNote, you can use the Lock All button in the Password Protection pane, or alternatively, you can use the CTRL+ALT+L key combination.

TIP Secure Passwords

In Microsoft OneNote, you can use up to 16 characters in your password. For best results, you should have at least one uppercase letter, one lowercase letter, one number, and one symbol, such as the colon (:). Using a pass phrase can help you more easily remember the password, and will make it harder to guess. A ***pass phrase*** is a string of words, such as mylonglostfriend. However, using camel case, a method that capitalizes each word in a phrase, would be better. MyLongLostFriend would make a better password. MyLongLostFriend1; (with the semi-colon on the end) would be an even better password. For best results, avoid words found in the dictionary. You can still use a pass phrase, just use the first letter or two of each word. Using the same example, you might use MyLoLoFr1;.

Add Tags

STEP 4 ***Tags*** are electronic markers you can add to your content to help with searches and organization of your notes. OneNote has 29 default tags, including To Do, Important, Question, Idea, and Critical. When these tags are added to individual notes, it provides quick access to specific information through the Find Tags command. The Find Tags command opens the Tags Summary pane, which lists the tags in the notebook. Simply scroll through the listed tags until you find the tag or tags you are looking for.

To add a tag to content:

1. Highlight the note or content you want to tag.
2. Click on the HOME tab.
3. In the Tags group, click the More button (a down arrow with a horizontal line above it—see Figure 2.6) to display the default tags.
4. Select the tag you want to use.

Tags can be stacked, too. For instance, in your class notes, you might have information the instructor mentions will be on an exam. You can highlight the information, and then add the Important and Remember for later tags. In a business environment, you might tag a new client's name with the Important and Contact tags. If you click the wrong tag when you are selecting the tag, click it again to turn it off. Tags are ***toggle commands***, meaning they are either on or off. Click a tag once and it turns on and displays the icon or highlighting selected. Click the same tag again, and it turns off, removing the tag from your note.

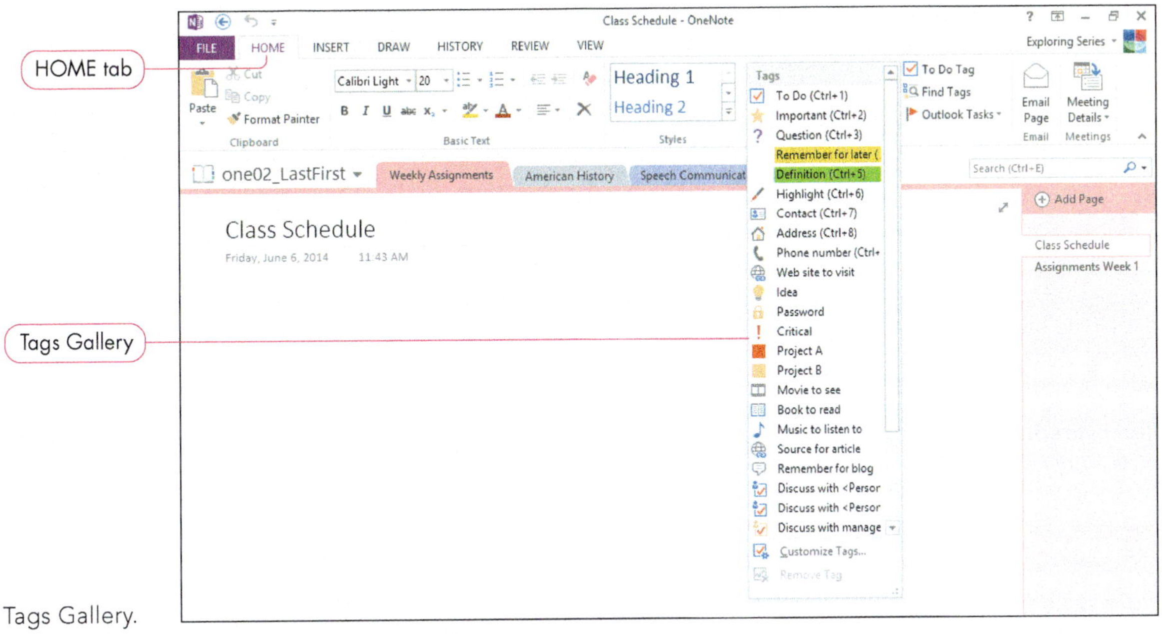

FIGURE 2.6 The Tags Gallery.

Search Notes

STEP 5» Searching for specific content in a notebook could be frustrating, if the notebook has several months or even years of notes in it. The search bar enables you to key a ***search term***, a phrase or keyword relevant to the content you are trying to find, and then select which notebook or section to search for the specified information. To search for specific notes or key terms:

1. In the search bar, type the search term.
2. Click the down arrow.
3. Select the search scope.

   A results pane appears listing all locations of the search term in the selected search scope.

Find Tags

Another way to search for and find specific content in a notebook is to use the ***Find Tags*** command. Located in the Tags group on the HOME tab, the Find Tags command gives you the option to search a page, section, notebook, or all notebooks on your storage device. To use the Find Tags command:

1. On the HOME tab, in the Tags group, click Find Tags.
2. In the Tags Summary pane, select a grouping category.
3. In the Search criteria box, select the page, section, notebook, or other area to search.
4. Click the desired tag link to navigate to the tag location in the notebook.

Quick Concepts

1. What is the advantage of using a page template instead of creating your own page design? ***p. 48***
2. Give three examples of when you would use the commands on the Review tab. ***pp. 50–51***
3. Why is using a pass phrase a good idea? Give an example of a pass phrase that would be difficult to guess. ***p. 52***
4. Explain three instances when you would add tags to your notebook content. ***p. 52***

Hands-On Exercises

1 Use Tools and Templates

After reviewing her notebook, Becky has decided it needs some color and design to make the information more memorable. You will help her learn to add formatting to her text, apply a page template to make her notes pages more useful, create a page template, check spelling, and use a thesaurus to find the correct word. You will also help her learn to research a topic from within OneNote, apply a password, search her notes, and add tags to her notes.

Skills covered: Format Text, Apply a Page Template, and Create a Template • Check Spelling, Use Thesaurus, and Research a Topic • Apply a Password • Search Notes • Add Tags

STEP 1 » FORMAT TEXT, APPLY A PAGE TEMPLATE, AND CREATE A TEMPLATE

In this section, you will format text previously added to the notebook in Chapter 1 Hands-On Exercises 1 and 2. To enhance the visual design and usefulness of pages, you will apply a different page template to several pages, and create a new template for use in the Assignments section. Refer to Figures 2.7 through 2.8 as you complete Step 1.

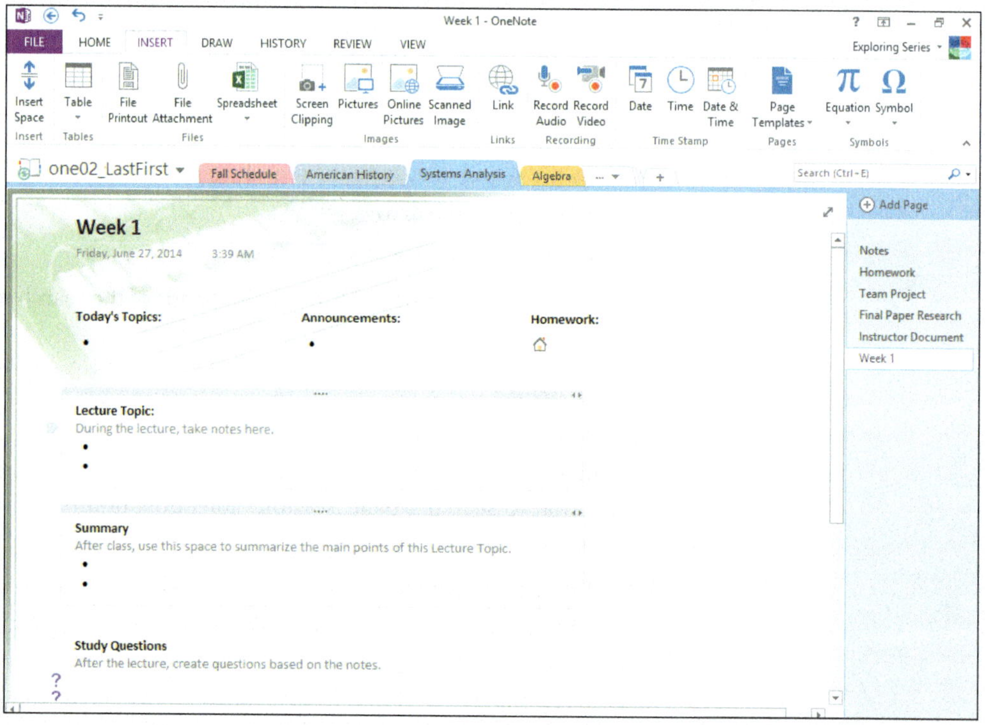

FIGURE 2.7 A page is added using the Academic Lecture Notes and Study Questions template.

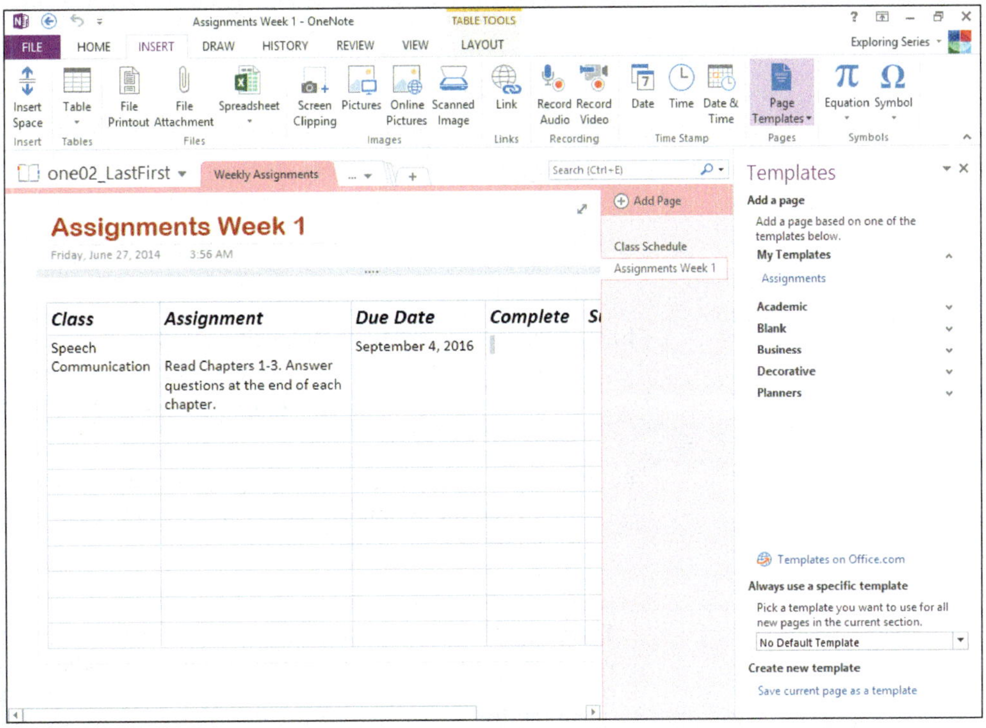

FIGURE 2.8 A new template named Assignments is created.

a. Open Word and navigate to your student data files. Open **one02h1_UseTools.docx**. If necessary, click **Enable Editing**. Type **your name**, below the subtitle, and then press **Enter**. Type the **current date** and then press **Enter** twice. Save the Word file as **one02h1_UseTools_LastFirst**.

b. Open **one01ClassNotebook_LastFirst** in OneNote. Export one01_LastFirst to your storage media as a .onepkg file named **one02_LastFirst**. Close **one01_LastFirst**. Open *one02_LastFirst*. Click on the **Notes** page, in the Systems Analysis section, and then highlight the Notes page title. Click the Font arrow, on the HOME tab, in the Basic Text group. Change the font to **Arial Rounded MT Bold**. Change the font color to **Red, Darker 25%**. With the title selected, click the **Format Painter** in the Clipboard group on the HOME tab twice to turn on the Format Painter.

c. Click the **American History** Section tab and then click the **Notes** Page tab. Drag the Format Painter pointer to select the page title and format the title. Click the **Notes** Page tab in the Speech Communication section. Drag the pointer across the page title to format the title. Use the Format Painter to make this change to the title on the Notes page in the Algebra section. Click the **Format Painter** once to turn it off.

d. Click the **Systems Analysis** Section tab. Click the bottom half of **Page Templates** in the Pages group on the INSERT tab, and then click **Page Templates** at the bottom of the list. Click **Academic** in the Templates pane, and then click **Lecture Notes and Study Questions**. Title the new page **Week 1**. Repeat these steps to add the **History class notes** template page to the American History tab, and the **Math/Science class notes** template page to the Algebra tab, and title them both **Week 1**. Close the Templates pane.

e. Click on the **Week 1 page** in the Systems Analysis Section tab. Take a **Full-screen Snip** using the **Snipping Tool**. Maximize Word. Paste the snip below the date. Save and minimize Word.

f. Rename the Fall Schedule Section tab as **Weekly Assignments**. Add a page and then Rename the Untitled page as **Assignments Week 1**. Highlight the **page title** on the Assignments Week 1 page. Change the font to **Arial Rounded MT Bold**. Change the font color to **Red, Darker 25%**. Click below the date and press **Enter**.

g. Type the following, pressing **Tab** after each, and then pressing **Enter** after Submitted:

   Class

   Assignment

   Due Date

   Complete

   Submitted

   Use the **Insert Below** command on the LAYOUT tab in the Insert group to add nine more rows of table cells.

h. Highlight the first row of table cells with the column headings, and change the font to **Bold** and **Italic**, and the font size to **16 pt**. Select all remaining cells below the first row, and change the font size to **12 pt**. You should have ten rows below the title row, which makes a total of eleven rows.

i. Place your pointer on the right edge of the table border to display a left and right pointing arrow. Hold the left mouse button and drag the edge to the right until all table headings are on a single line.

> **TROUBLESHOOTING:** Depending on which edge you place the pointer, the double arrow will be white with a black outline or black with two vertical lines between the arrows. Place your pointer on the edge that has the black double arrow with two vertical lines between the arrows.

j. Click the **INSERT tab**, and then click top half of the **Page Templates** button in the Pages group. Click **Save current page as a template** at the bottom of the Templates pane. Type **Assignments** in the Template name text box, in the **Save As** Template dialog box, and then click **Save**.

k. Click in the first cell below the Class heading. Type **Speech Communication**, and then press **Tab**. Type **Read Chapters 1–3. Answer questions at the end of each chapter.** Press **Tab**, and then type **September 4, 2016**. Resize columns as needed to display contents. See Figure 2.8.

l. Click **My Templates**, in the Templates pane. Use the **Snipping Tool** to create a **Full-screen Snip**. Maximize Word. **Paste** the snip below the previous snip. **Save** and minimize Word. Close the Templates pane.

STEP 2 » CHECK SPELLING, USE A THESAURUS, AND RESEARCH A TOPIC

To make sure she has not inadvertently added spelling mistakes to her notebook, Becky has asked you to help her check spelling. She would also like to use the thesaurus to replace a word and research a topic using the research tools built into OneNote. Refer to Figures 2.9 through 2.11 as you complete Step 2.

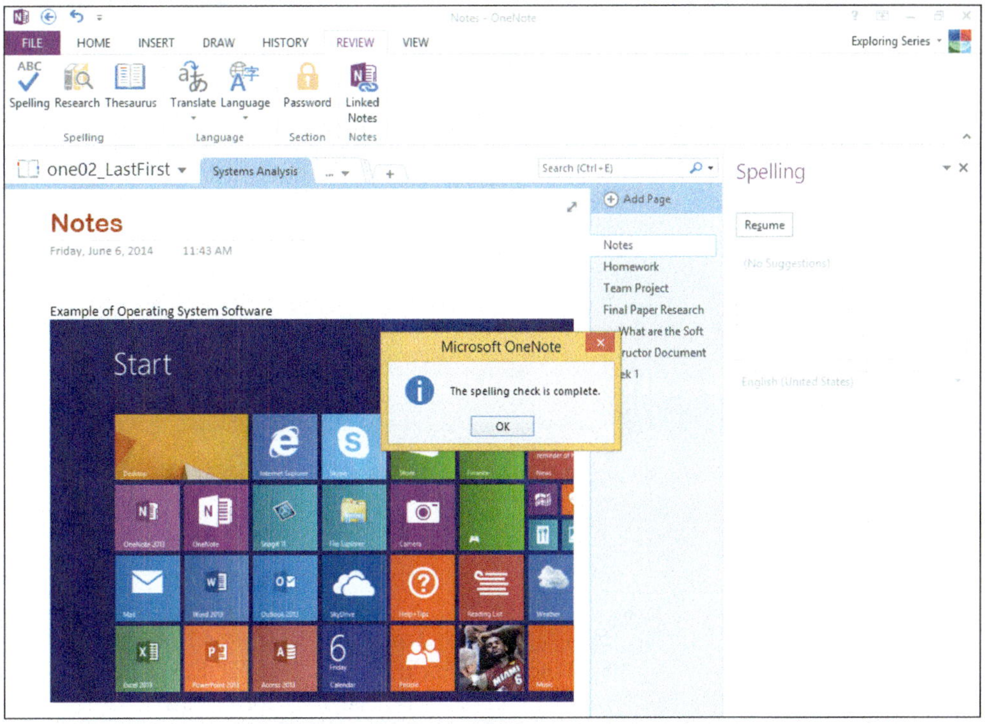

FIGURE 2.9 Microsoft OneNote displays a message after a spelling check is completed.

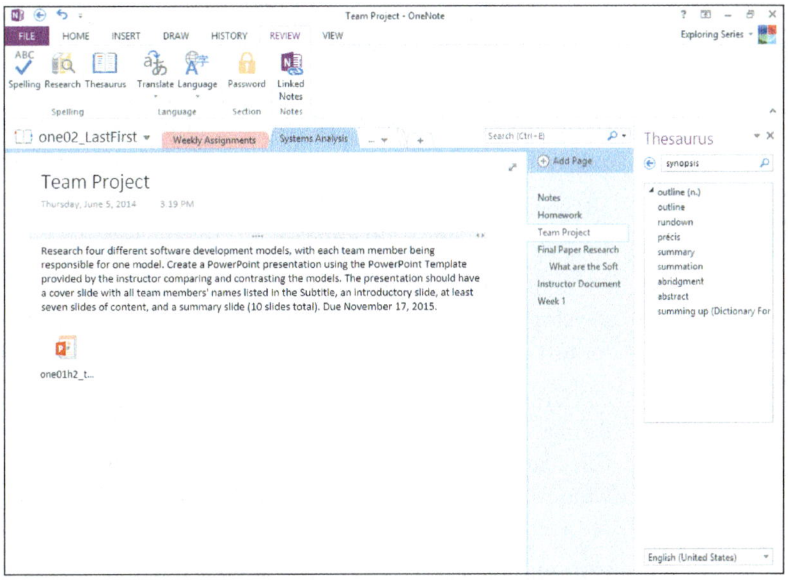

FIGURE 2.10 The word 'synopsis' is changed to 'summary' using OneNote's Thesaurus.

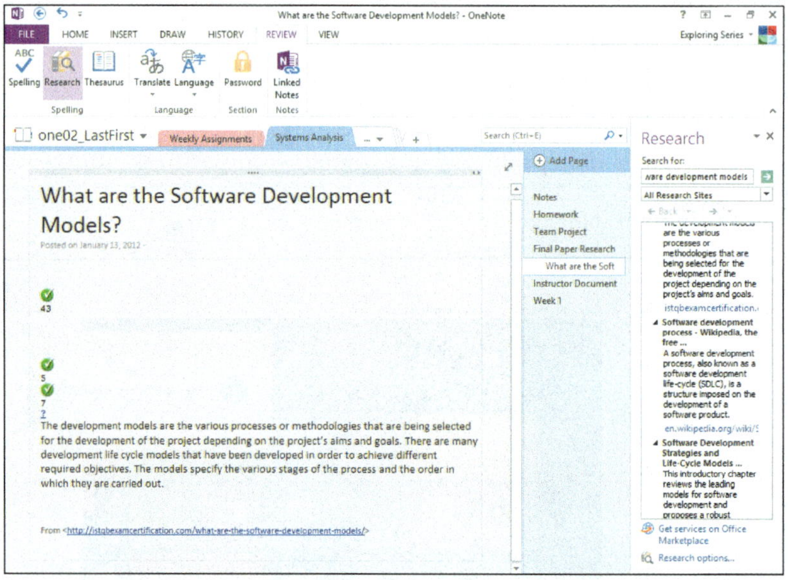

FIGURE 2.11 Using the Research pane to research a topic.

a. Navigate to the **Systems Analysis section Notes page**. Click the **REVIEW tab**, and then click **Spelling**, in the Spelling group to check the spelling in the Systems Analysis section. Ignore the word Abend, and accept all other corrections, if needed.

b. Use the **Snipping Tool** to take a **Full-screen Snip**, with the message, The spelling check is complete, still on the screen. Maximize Word. Paste the snip below the previous snip. **Save** and minimize Word.

c. Highlight the word **synopsis**, on the Systems Analysis Team section Project page, and then click **Thesaurus**, in the Spelling group. Find ***summary*** in the Thesaurus pane, in the list of suggested words. Click the down arrow, and then click **Insert**.

d. Use the **Snipping Tool** to take a **Full-screen Snip**. Maximize Word. Paste the snip below the previous snip. Save and minimize Word.

e. Close the Thesaurus pane. Click **Research**, in the Spelling group, and then type **software development models**, in the Search for text box. Click the **down arrow**, below the Search for text box, and then select **All Research Sites**. If necessary, click **Start Searching**.

f. Click the **hyperlink** below any one of the search return items, avoiding all Wikipedia.org listings. Maximize the browser. Highlight and copy the title and first paragraph of text. Click **Send to OneNote**, in the taskbar. Click **New Quick Note (N)**. Right-click in the note window, and then click the first icon below **Paste** (Keep Source Formatting (K)). Close the browser.

g. Click the **Notebook pane tab** (the arrow to the left of the first Section tab), in OneNote. Scroll to the bottom of the notebook file list and then click **Quick Notes**. Right-click on the tab for the page you just copied into Quick Note. Click **Move or Copy**. **Expand** the **one02_LastFirst** notebook, and then click **Systems Analysis**. Click **Move**.

h. Drag the new Page tab to move the page below the **Final Research Paper** page.

i. Right-click the tab of the new page, and then click **Make Subpage**.

j. Use the **Snipping Tool** to take a **Full-screen Snip**. Maximize Word. Paste the snip below the previous snip. Save and minimize Word. Close the Research pane

STEP 3 》 APPLY A PASSWORD

Becky wants to add some personal information to her notebook. After she creates the Personal section, she asks you to help her password protect the section containing her personal information. Refer to Figure 2.12 as you complete Step 3.

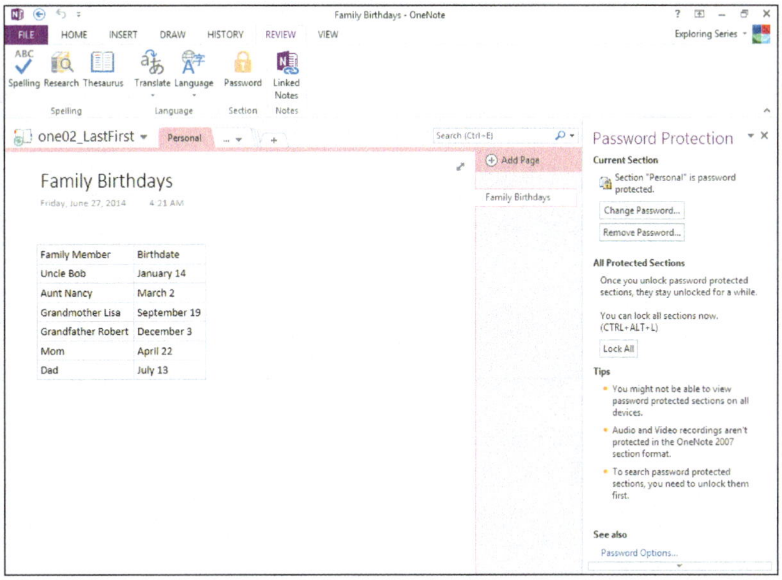

FIGURE 2.12 A table of family birthdays has been added to the Personal section Family Birthdays page.

a. Add a new section titled **Personal**. Name the Untitled pate **Family Birthdays**.

b. Type **Family Member** on the Family Birthdays page below the date, press **Tab** and then type **Birthdate**. Press **Enter**. Type **Uncle Bob**, press **Tab**, type **January 14**, and then press **Enter**. Type **Aunt Nancy**, press **Tab**, and then type **March 2**. Continue to add the following information to the table:

   Grandmother Lisa—September 19

   Grandfather Robert—December 3

   Mom—April 22

   Dad—July 13

c. Click **Password** in the **Section group** on the **REVIEW tab**, and then click **Set Password** in the Password Protection pane. Type **OneNote** in the Enter Password text box, in the Password Protection pane, press Tab, and then retype **OneNote** in the Confirm Password text box. Click **OK**.

d. Use the **Snipping Tool** to take a **Full-screen Snip**. Maximize Word. Paste the snip below the previous snip. Save and minimize Word. Close the Password Protection pane.

STEP 4 》 ADD TAGS

With exams coming up, Becky has been reviewing her notes. She has decided to add tags to material the instructors have indicated will be on the tests, and wants to mark topics she needs help understanding. Refer to Figures 2.13 and 2.14 as you complete Step 4.

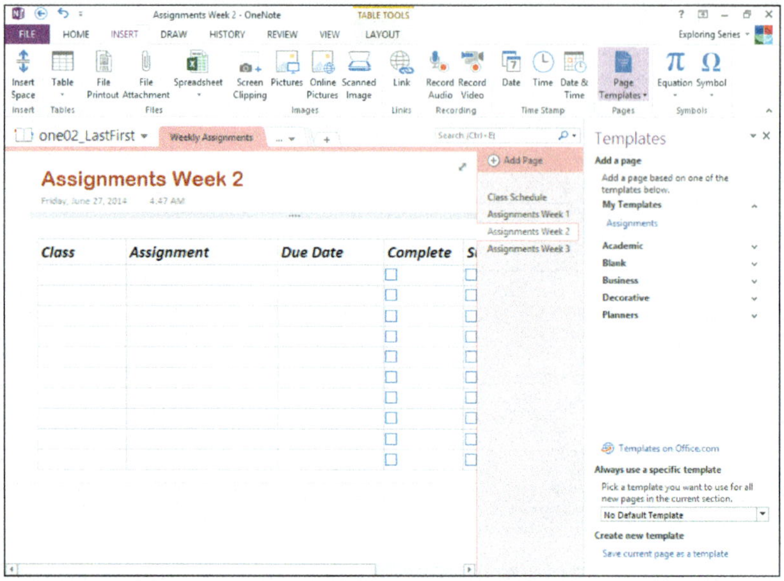

FIGURE 2.13 A new Assignments template page has To Do tags in the Complete and Submitted columns.

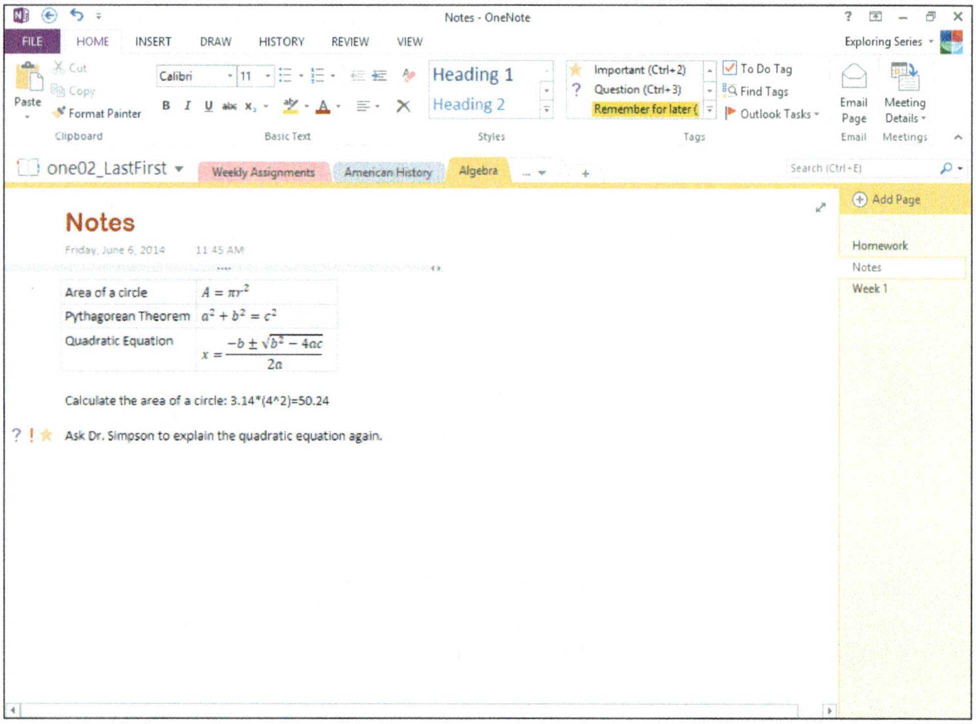

FIGURE 2.14 A table with formulas is inserted, and OneNote calculates the area of a circle.

a. On the Weekly Assignments Section tab Assignments Week 1 page, select the **Complete** and **Submitted** columns. Click the **To Do Tag** in the Tags group on the HOME tab to insert the tag in all the cells below Completed and Submitted.

b. On the first row below the table headings row, in the Complete and Submitted columns, click the **To Do tag check boxes** to indicate that this assignment has been completed and submitted.

c. Click the **INSERT tab**, and then click the bottom half of the **Page Template command**, in the Pages group, and then click Page Templates at the bottom of the list. Click **My Templates**. Right-click the **Assignments template name**, and then click **Delete**. Click **Save current page as a template**, at the bottom of the Template pane. Name the page template **Assignments**. Click **Save**.

d. Click **Assignments** below My Templates in the Templates pane to add two more Assignments Week 1 pages in the Weekly Assignments section. Apply the **Assignments template**, for each inserted page, and then **change the week number** until you have Assignments Week 1 through Assignments Week 3. For Assignments Week 2 and Assignments Week 3 pages, remove the Speech Communication Assignment from the table, and then click the To Do boxes on the first row to remove the checkmarks.

   As the semester progresses, Becky can add a new Assignments page for each week.

e. Click on **Assignments Week 2** Page tab. Use the **Snipping Tool** to take a **Full-screen Snip**. Maximize Word. Paste the snip below the previous snip. Save and minimize Word. Close the Templates pane.

f. Navigate to the **Algebra section Notes page**. Below the calculation type **Ask Dr. Simpson to explain the quadratic equation again.** Click before Ask in the sentence you just typed, and then in the Tags group on the HOME tab, click **Question (Ctrl+3)**. Click **More** on the Tags gallery, and then insert the **Critical tag**. Add an **Important tag** to indicate that this information will be on the exam.

g. Use the **Snipping Tool** to take a **Full-screen Snip**. Maximize Word. Paste the snip below the previous snip. Save and minimize Word.

STEP 5 » SEARCH NOTES

Becky needs to locate her notes on the quadratic equation, and also needs to locate the Important tags in her notebook to help her know what specific information to study. You will show her how to search her notes for specific information and tags. Refer to Figures 2.15 and 2.16 as you complete Step 5.

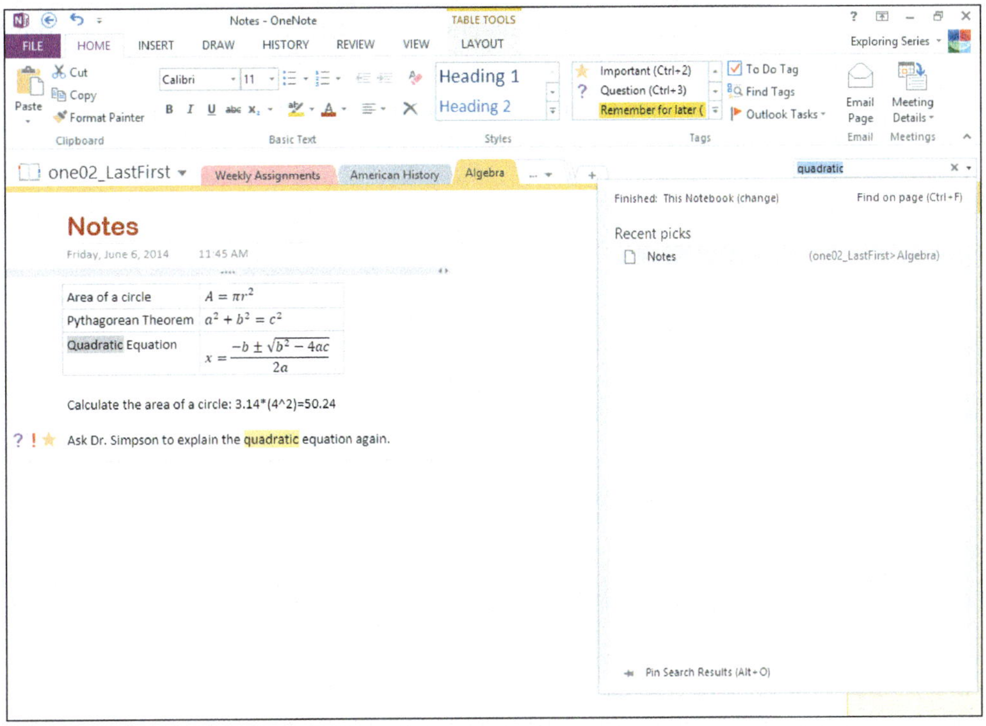

FIGURE 2.15 Search finds content in your notebook.

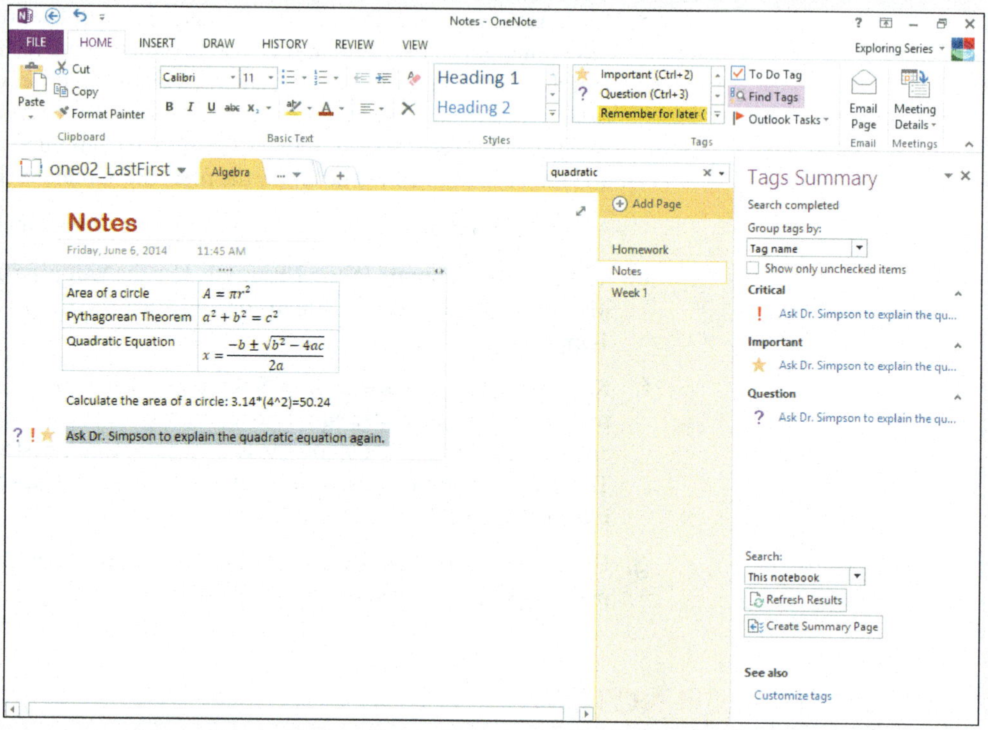

FIGURE 2.16 Tagged content can be located using the Find Tags command.

a. Click the **Systems Analysis** Section tab. Type **quadratic** in the Search box, and then click the arrow at the far right of the Search box. Click **This Notebook** to set the search scope, and then press **Enter**. If necessary, click on the link to the Algebra Notes page.

b. Use the **Snipping Tool** to take a **Full-screen Snip**. Maximize Word. Paste the snip below the previous snip. Save and minimize Word.

c. Click the **American History section Final Paper Research** Page tab. Click **Find Tags** in the Tags group on the HOME tab. Click the **arrow** below *Group tags by:* in the Tags Summary pane, make sure **Tag name** is displayed. Below *Search:* make sure **This notebook** is selected.

d. Click the link below **Critical.** Use the Snipping Tool to take a **Full-screen Snip**. Maximize Word. Paste the snip below the quadratic snip taken previously. Save and close Word. Submit the Word document as directed by your instructor.

Working Online and Collaborating with OneNote

OneDrive, formerly known as SkyDrive, is Microsoft's free web storage interface that also provides access to Microsoft Word, Excel, PowerPoint, and OneNote to people with a Microsoft account. These ***Online Apps*** are similar to the desktop versions, but have limited functionality. As an example, in the OneNote 2013 desktop version, you can record an audio file from within OneNote. In the OneNote Online app, you can insert or embed an audio recording, but you cannot create one. There are three ways to get a free Microsoft account to gain access to OneDrive. Visit one of the three links below, and follow directions to sign up.

- www.live.com
- www.OneDrive.com
- www.outlook.com

You can access OneDrive through any browser or from the Windows 8.1 Start screen. By default, the OneDrive app is installed with Windows 8.1. You may have to log into OneDrive the first time you use the OneDrive app, but after that, Windows 8.1 will automatically sign into OneDrive when you turn on the computer and the Windows operating system loads. If the OneDrive tile is not on your Start screen, click the All Programs (apps) button to see the list of available apps, right-click on the OneDrive tile, and then in the bar at the bottom of the screen, click Pin to Start.

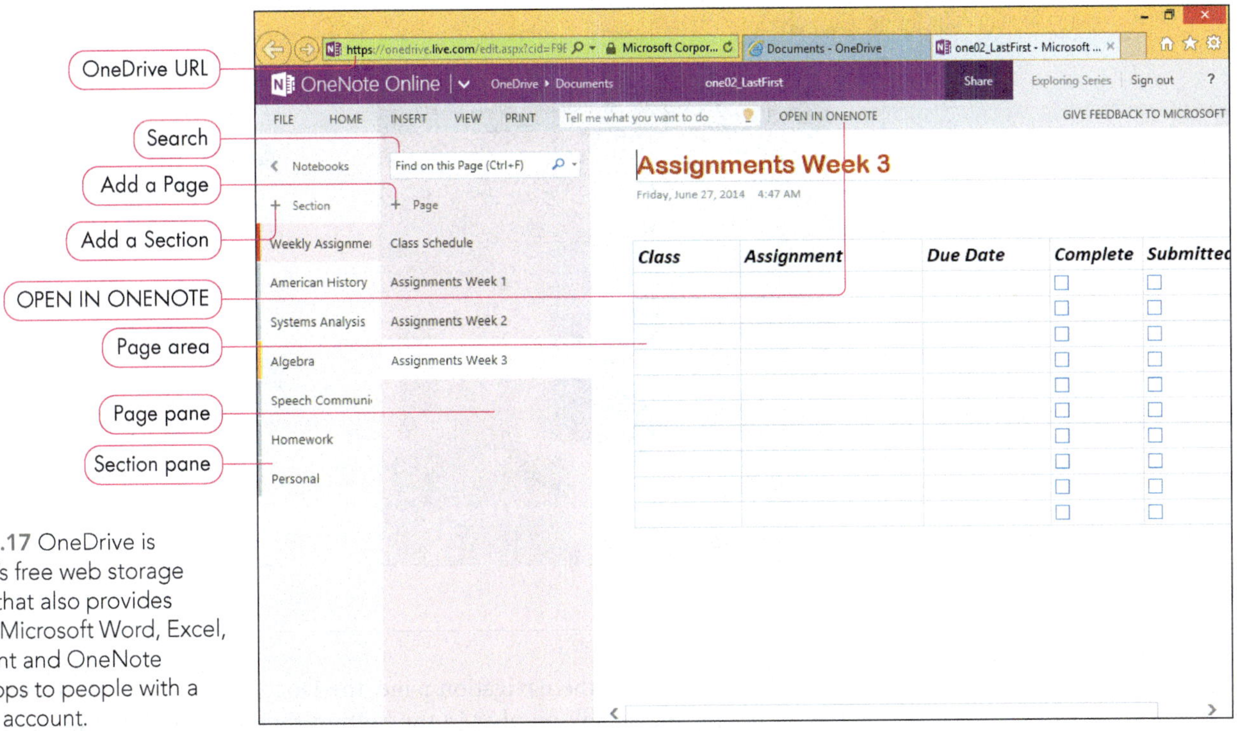

FIGURE 2.17 OneDrive is Microsoft's free web storage interface that also provides access to Microsoft Word, Excel, PowerPoint and OneNote Online Apps to people with a Microsoft account.

Use OneNote Online App

STEP 1 ›»

OneNote Online App is a limited function OneDrive version of OneNote 2013. The two versions seamlessly integrate through your browser. By saving your OneNote 2013 notebook on OneDrive, you ensure that you have access to your notebooks from any location with Internet access. This is particularly helpful for students and professionals alike, because you no longer have to carry your notes with you. With access to an Internet-connected device, you have access to your notes.

The OneNote Online App is a limited version of the desktop application, and it is immediately noticeable, because the online app interface differs from the OneNote desktop interface. If the Ribbon is minimized, click the Expand the Ribbon arrow below the Help (?) button in the top right corner of the screen. There are six tabs on the Online App Ribbon: FILE, HOME, INSERT, VIEW, PRINT, and OPEN IN ONENOTE. The navigation pane on the left contains all Section and Page tabs. There are no tabs on the right side of the screen.

Basic OneNote functions are available in the Online App, too, but may work in a slightly different manner. For instance, you would use the + Section command at the top of the Section tabs to add a section. Alternatively, you can either right-click an existing Section tab and then click New Section, or on the INSERT tab, in the Notebook group, click New Section. To add a new page, click + Page command above the Page tabs, or right-click on an existing Section tab or Page tab, and then click New Page. As an alternative, you can click New Page in the Notebook group on the INSERT tab. To name an New Section 1 tab or to rename a Section tab to another name, right-click on the tab, and then click Rename. To name an untitled page, click in the page title and type the title. This is the default page title.

To access files on your OneDrive, you can use the OneDrive tile or open a browser and navigate to www.OneDrive.com. If you have not accessed OneDrive previously, or if you have not logged into your Microsoft account, you will be presented with a log in screen. Type your Microsoft account e-mail and password, and then click Sign In. However, to use the Microsoft Office Online Apps, you will need to log in through your browser.

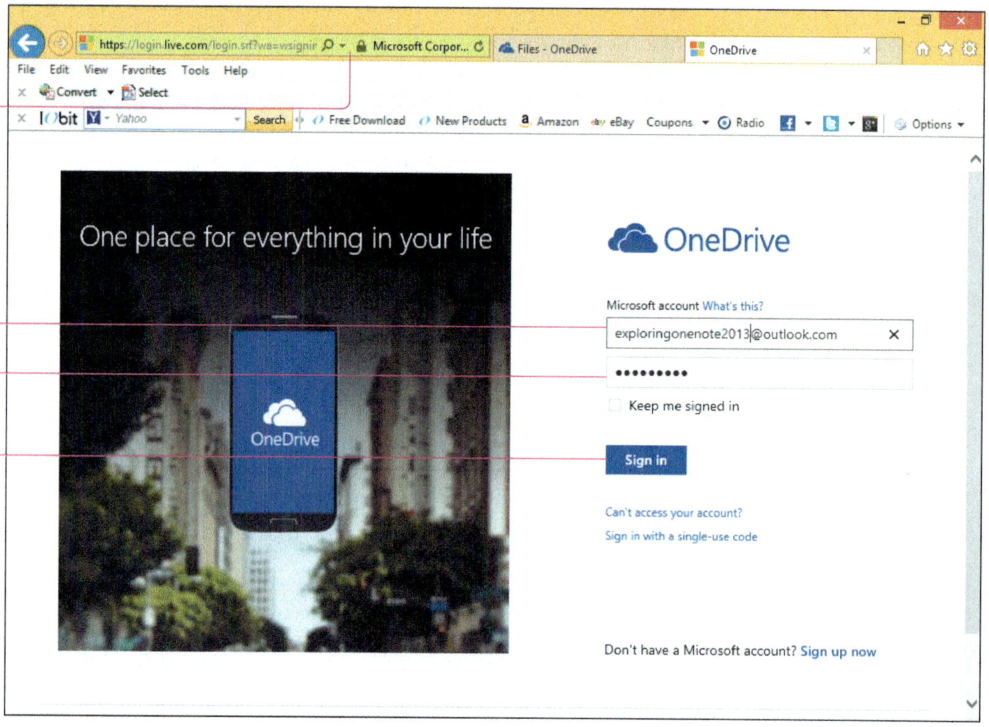

FIGURE 2.18 In your browser, navigate to www.OneDrive.com to create a OneDrive account.

With Files selected in the navigation pane, the Documents folder tile displays. If there are files in the folder, a small number in the bottom right corner gives the number of files included in the folder. Files in this OneDrive folder are accessible from the File Explorer window in Windows 8.1, as long as you are signed into OneDrive and have Internet access.

To create a notebook in OneNote Online App:

1. In the top menu bar, click the Create button.
2. Click OneNote notebook.
3. Type a name for the new notebook in the New Microsoft OneNote notebook dialog box.
4. Click Create or press Enter.

To access an existing OneNote notebook in OneDrive, click the Documents folder tile and then click the filename of the file.

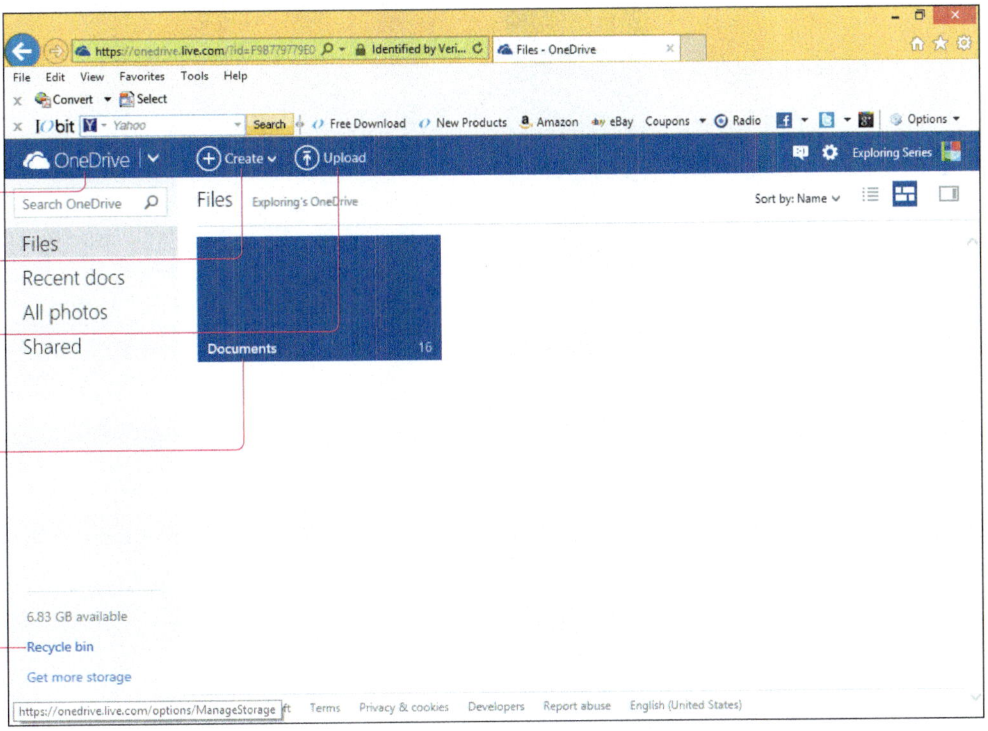

FIGURE 2.19 The OneDrive Documents folder.

Create Sections and Pages in OneNote Online App

The OneNote Online App interface differs from the OneNote 2013 desktop interface. The Section pane is on the far left side of the screen. Just to the right of the Section pane is the Page pane. The Ribbon is hidden until you click on HOME, INSERT, VIEW, or PRINT tabs. The FILE tab opens Backstage view, and the OPEN IN ONENOTE opens the current Online App notebook in your desktop OneNote 2013. When you first create a Online App notebook, the notebook opens with one untitled section, which has one untitled page.

To rename an existing Section tab in OneNote Online App:

1. Right-click the Section tab.
2. Click Rename.
3. Type the new section name.
4. Click OK.

To add a section in OneNote Online App:

1. In the Section pane, click + Section.
2. Type a name for the section.
3. Click OK.

To rename a page:

1. On the page, select the title.
2. Press Delete.
3. Type the new page title.

You cannot upload a file to a page in the Online App, because the OneNote Online App is limited. However, you can use the OPEN IN ONENOTE tab to open the Online App notebook in your desktop OneNote 2013 application. At this point, you have the full capability of the desktop version for the notebook. Make the changes you need and sync the notebook to save those changes to the OneDrive notebook.

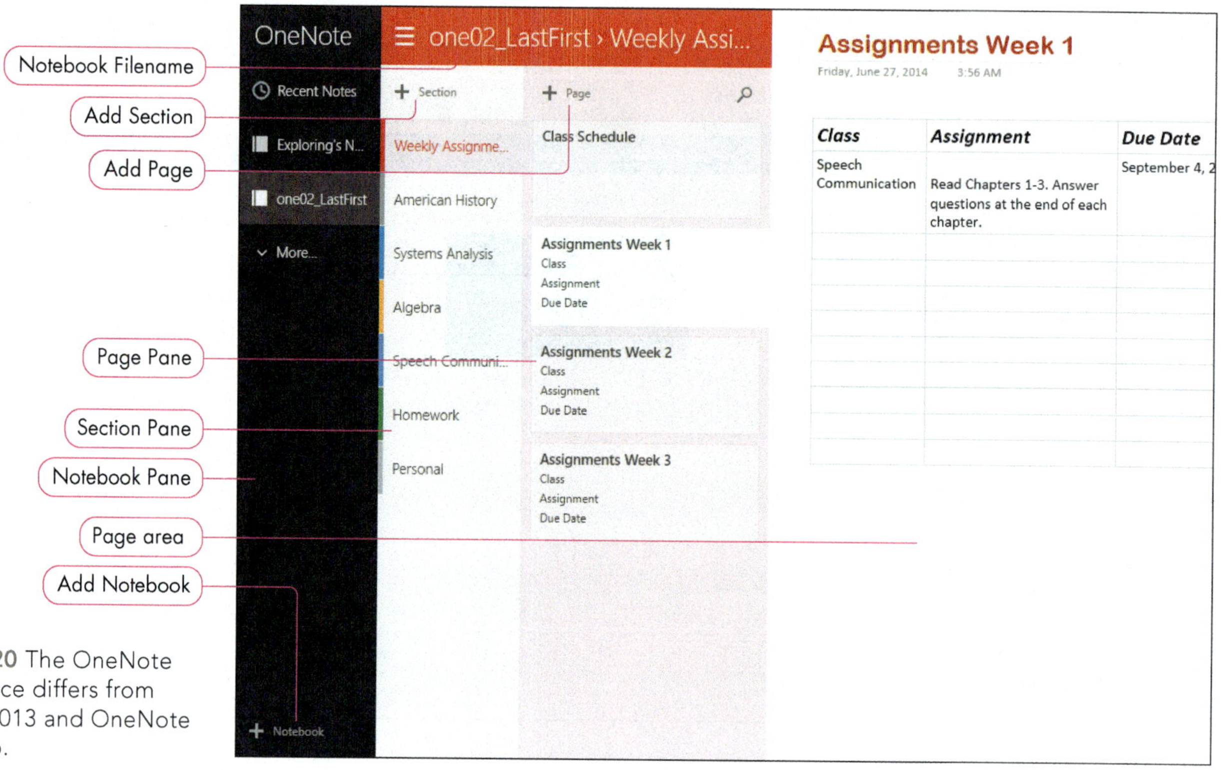

FIGURE 2.20 The OneNote App interface differs from OneNote 2013 and OneNote Online App.

Synchronize OneNote 2013 with OneNote Online App

STEP 2»

To save changes made in your desktop OneNote application notebook to your OneDrive Online App notebook, you ***sync*** the two to make them the same. How you sync your OneNote notebooks depends on whether you are in the desktop application or the Online App. To sync your notebooks when you are working in the desktop application, follow these steps:

1. In OneNote 2013, click the FILE tab.
2. If necessary, click Info.
3. Click View Sync Status.
4. To the right of the notebook name, click the Sync Now button. If necessary, sign in again.

At the top of the Shared Notebook Synchronization dialog box, you have the choice to Sync automatically whenever there are changes or Sync manually. If you sync automatically, you never have to worry about not having the same information on all versions of your notebook.

To sync your notebooks when you are working in the OneNote Online App, click the OPEN IN ONENOTE tab. The notebook will reopen in the desktop application. Depending on your browser, you may have to re-enter your e-mail and password. After you make changes or add content to the notebook, sync the notebook so that the changes will be uploaded back to the Online App.

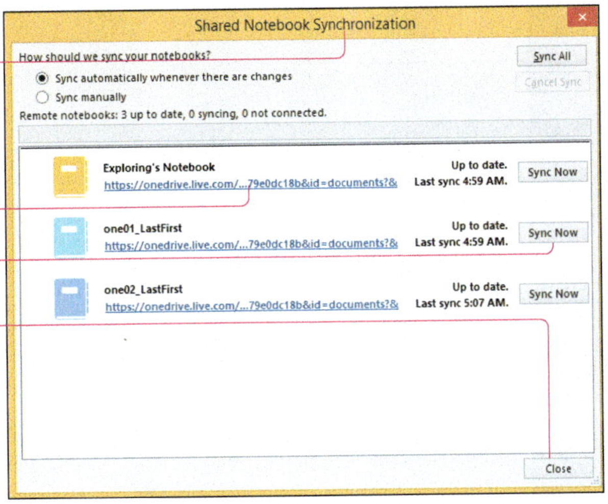

FIGURE 2.21 The Shared Notebook Synchronization dialog box syncs your notebook to OneNote Online App and OneNote App.

Share a Notebook

STEP 3

OneNote notebooks can be shared with anyone with OneNote or the OneNote Online App access, even if they are using iOS or Android systems. The ability to ***share*** notebooks with fellow workers, students, or family is a powerful feature allowing teams or groups to collaborate on projects. For instance, opening a OneNote notebook saved to OneDrive during an online meeting via a chat using an application such as Lync or Skype, enables you to share the notebook with everyone in the meeting.

To share your OneNote 2013 desktop notebook:

1. Open the notebook on your desktop.
2. Click the FILE tab, and then click Share.
3. Select a sharing option:
   - Invite People,
   - Get a Sharing Link,
   - Share with Meeting,
   - Move Notebook.

Invite People lets you send e-mails to multiple individuals and select what permissions they have, either View or View and Edit. Though you can select multiple individuals, you can only select one permissions level. If you need some people to have the ability to edit the notebook, you will need to send more than one Invite People e-mail. You can also choose whether users are required to log in with a Microsoft account. Note that if you choose this option, users without a Microsoft account will not be able to log in.

The *Get a Sharing Link* option enables you to get a link that can be shared with users on social networks, such as Twitter or Facebook. You can also send the link in an online chat, an e-mail, or post it in a Web page or blog. Select the View link or the Edit link, depending on the permissions needed by the users. View permissions enable users to look at notebook pages and sections, but not to make changes. Edit permissions enable users to both look at and make changes to notebook pages and sections. Sharing the link on publicly available sites may be against company policy.

The *Share with Meeting* shares the notebook with a meeting set up in Outlook. This is beyond the scope of this book. To learn more about sharing a notebook with a meeting set up in Outlook, search for information in your browser, or visit **http://www.youtube.com/watch?v=IucFH3NVII0**.

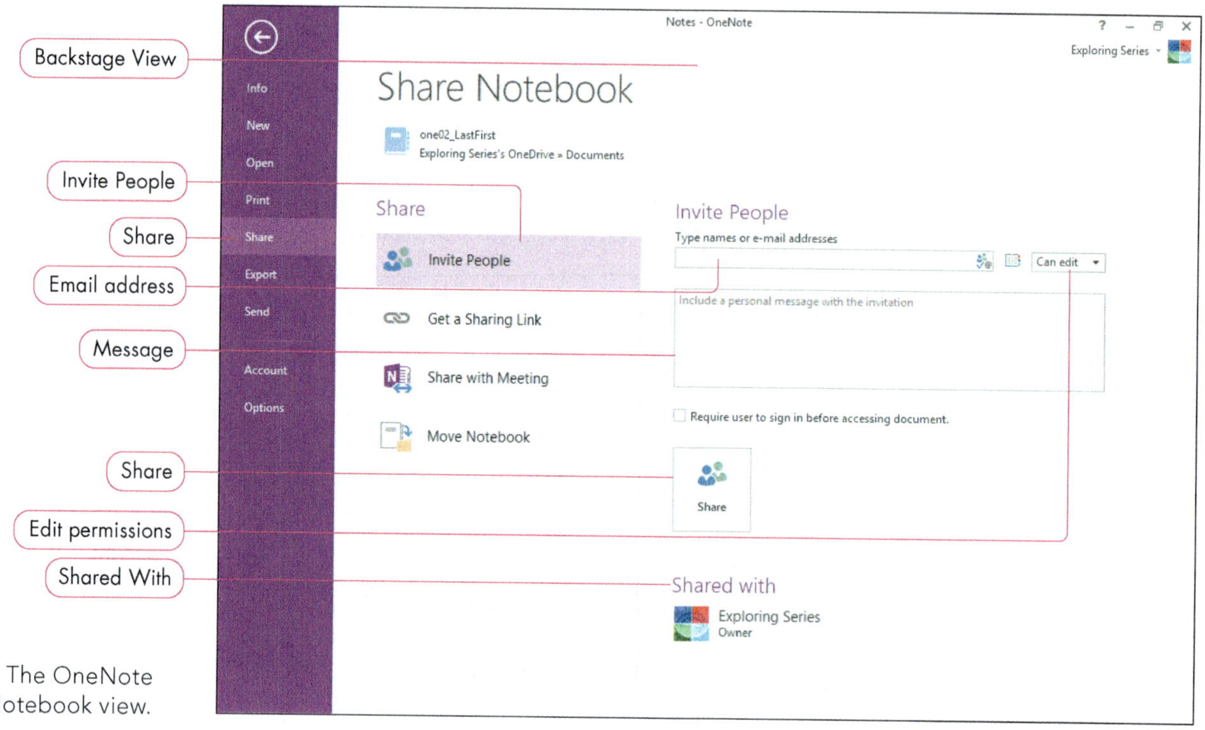

FIGURE 2.22 The OneNote 2013 Share Notebook view.

Once you have shared a notebook, it should not be moved to a new location on your hard drive or server. This breaks the path, the route the user's computer follows to find the notebook file, which causes the share not to work. The Move Notebook option in the Share window explains in more detail the issues involved in moving shared notebooks.

To share your OneNote Online App notebook:

1. Click the FILE tab.
2. Click Share.
3. Click Share with People button.
4. In the Share dialog box, if necessary, select Invite people.
5. In the To text box, type an e-mail address.
6. Type a note in the Add a quick note text box.
7. Select Recipients can edit or Recipients can only view.
8. If you are requiring users to sign in to their Microsoft accounts before accessing the notebook, check the Require user to sign in before accessing document check box.
9. Click Share.

To send the invitation to more than one person, after typing the first e-mail address, press the semi-colon key (;) and type the next e-mail address. By typing a semi-colon after each e-mail address, you can invite multiple people to share the notebook.

If you want to share the OneNote Online App notebook to a group, you can create a link that you can copy and paste into an e-mail, blog, or Web page. Users click the link to open the notebook. To create this link:

1. Click the FILE tab.
2. Click Share.
3. Click Share with People button.
4. In the Share dialog box, select Get a link.
5. Select a sharing option.
   - View Only—enables person to view the notebook, but not make changes to it
   - Edit—enables the person to make changes to the notebook
   - Public—opens the notebook for anyone with the link to open and view it
6. Click Create link

7. Copy the link
8. Paste the link in the e-mail, blog, or Web page.

It is important to select the appropriate options when using this Get a link method. The View only option enables anyone with the link to see the files you share. If you select the Public option, anyone can search for and view your public files, even without having the link. With the Edit option, everyone who uses the link has edit permissions to your notebook.

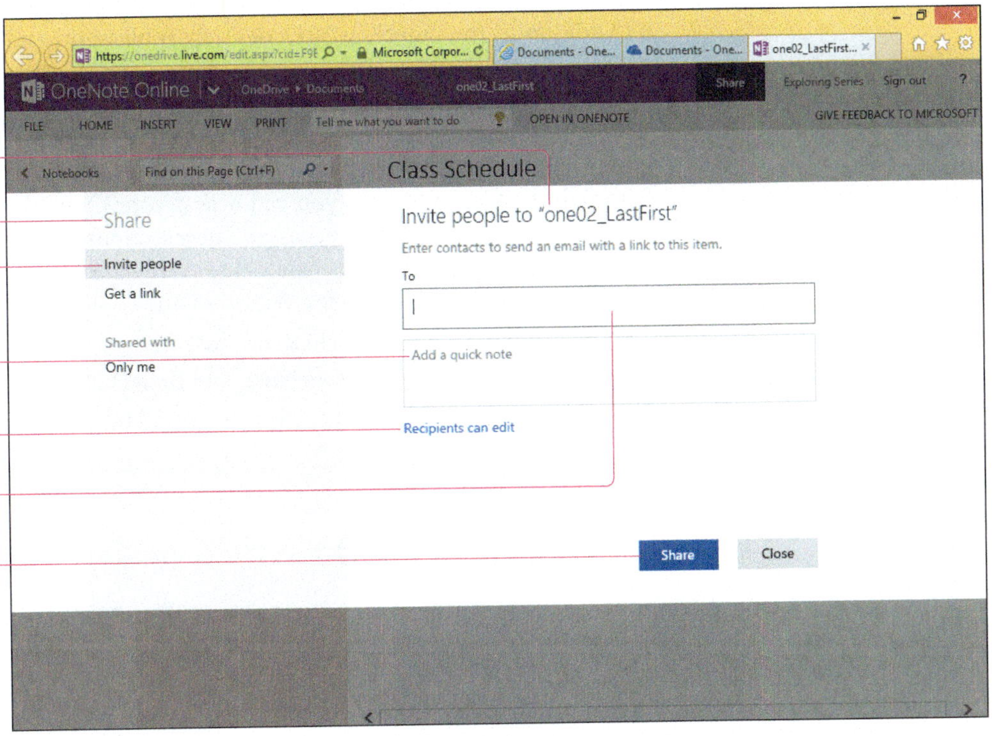

FIGURE 2.23 The OneNote Online App sharing view.

Use Version Control and Track Multiple Authors

STEP 4

In OneNote 2013, the HISTORY tab provides access to review all changes made to the notebook, even if those changes were made by someone else with whom you have shared the notebook. The Unread group contains commands to help you locate changes you have not yet seen, and then mark them as read. In the Authors group, the Recent Edits lets you check for changes made Today, Since Yesterday, Last 7 Days, and up to the Last 6 Months. This is really helpful if several people are working in the notebook, and made changes that need to be undone. You can search through a section, section group, a notebook, or even all notebooks, to find changes made by a specific author. The Hide Authors command hides the author information. It is a toggle button, so to show the author information again, simply click the Hide Authors command again.

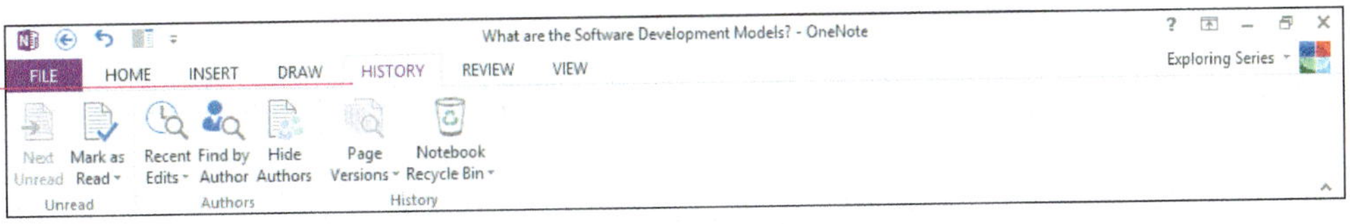

FIGURE 2.24 The HISTORY tab.

The History group contains the Page Versions and the Notebook Recycle Bin commands. Once a version has been reviewed and approved, previous versions can be deleted using the Page Versions down arrow. The Notebook Recycle Bin holds all deleted pages, sections, and notebooks until the recycle bin is emptied, or for 60 days, whichever comes first. To move a page or section out of the Recycle Bin, right-click the page name, click Move or Copy, and move it to the notebook. Using either of the History group commands, you can completely disable history for a specific notebook. Because the Recycle Bin acts as a safety net that enables you to retrieve accidentally deleted pages and section, you should consider very carefully before disabling the history.

In the OneNote Online App, the HISTORY tab is not available. To see the versions and authors, you must use the VIEW tab. The Page Versions command displays a list of all versions available in the Online App. Versions cannot be discarded in the Online App.

Installing and Using Windows 8.1 OneNote App

STEP 5» In addition to the OneNote 2013 desktop application and the OneDrive OneNote Online App, there is a ***OneNote App*** you can add to your Windows 8.1 on your pc, your tablet, or your compatible smartphone. The Windows 8.1 OneNote App is a free app available through the Windows Store that is primarily designed for touch screens on tablets and smartphones. Controls are larger, because fingers will be utilized to navigate the screen and select commands. Through the OneNote App, you can access your OneDrive OneNote Online App to make quick additions to your notes pages, add new sections or pages, or even create a new notebook. When you sync the files, your changes are saved back to your OneNote Online App notebook.

To get the OneNote App for Windows 8.1:

1. From your Start screen, click the Store tile.
2. In the Search box, type OneNote, and then click the OneNote link.
3. On the OneNote app page, click the Install button.

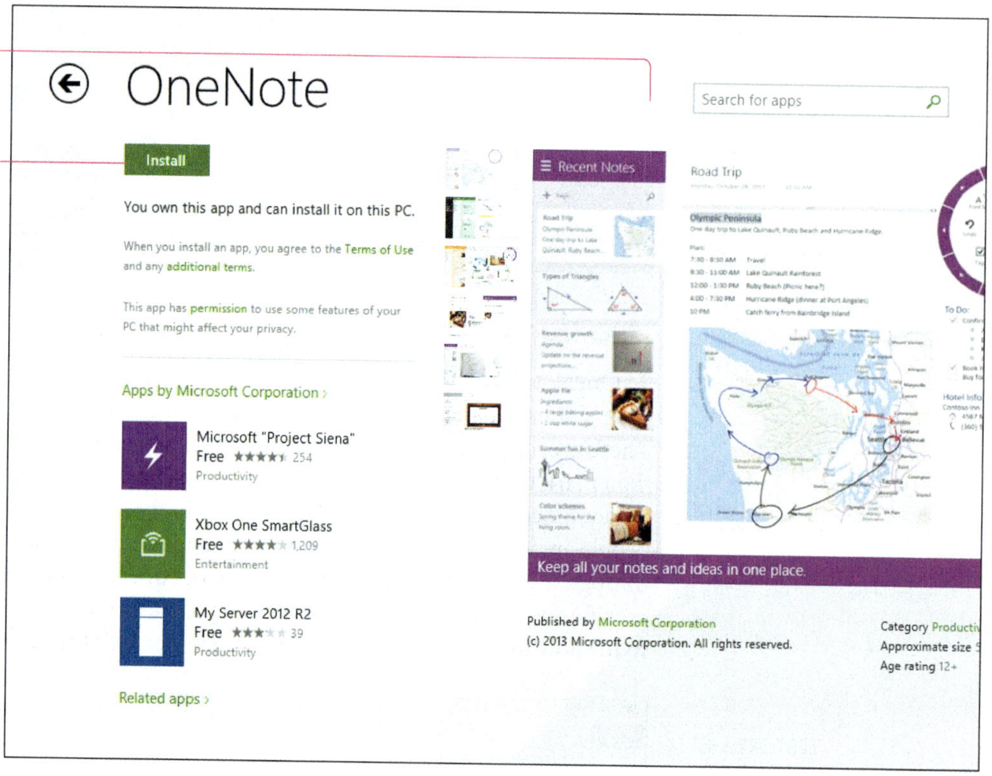

FIGURE 2.25 The OneNote App is available through the Windows 8.1 Store.

FIGURE 2.26 The OneNote App and OneNote 2013 tiles.

The amount of time it takes to download and install to your system depends on your Internet connection. After the app installs, pin the OneNote tile to your Start screen, then click the tile. You will have to set up the app before you can use it. If you use the Express Set Up button, the app will access your system's OneNote 2013 application information to configure the app to work with your existing OneNote desktop installation. The user interface of the Online App is different than that of the desktop application. When OneNote opens, the most recently opened notebook displays open on the screen. To change the section or notebook, click Quick Notes. The far left navigation pane lists your notebooks, the next navigation pane to the right lists the sections in the selected notebook, and the third navigation pane lists the pages in the selected section.

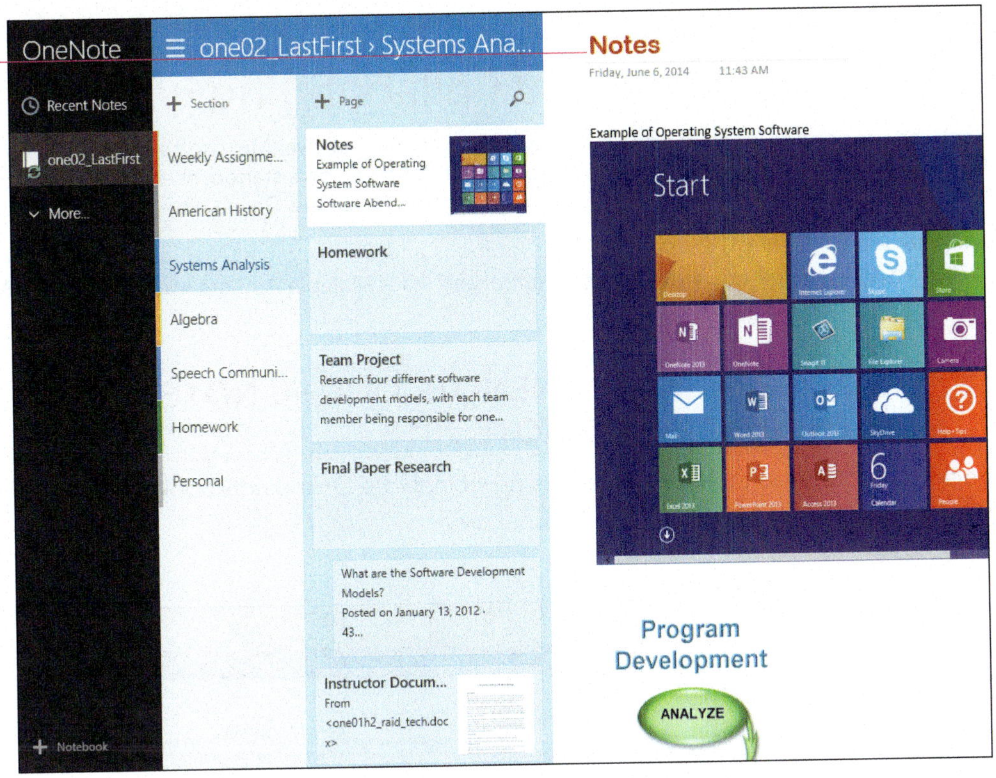

FIGURE 2.27 The OneNote App interface.

You can add a notebook by clicking the + Notebook command at the bottom of the Notebook navigation pane. To add a section, click the + Section button at the top of the Section Pane. To add a page, click the + Page button at the top of the Page pane. To rename a section, right-click the current name. In the menu at the bottom of the screen, select Rename Section. Other options available for working with sections in the menu include Delete Section, Section Color, Copy Link to Section, and Pin to Start. Right-clicking a page name opens a menu at the bottom of the page with Delete Page, Rename Page, Subpages, Copy Link to Page, and Pin to Start buttons. However, to delete a notebook, you will need to use the desktop version or OneDrive Online App.

To insert content into a page, select the page, then click in the page where you want to add content or type. A radial menu button appears. Click on the button to open the main radial menu. A complete explanation of how to use radial menus is outside the scope of this book. If you have a touch screen tablet and wish to learn to use the radial menus, and take a virtual tour of OneNote for Windows 8.1, visit **http://www.youtube.com/watch?v=hTOkeH5VZXQ**. Alternatively, you can search for OneNote for Windows 8.1 to find more videos.

The exact method for installation of OneNote to smartphones and tablets may vary. To get started, open your App Store or Market Place. Search for OneNote. If your phone is compatible, follow the on-screen directions to install. If your phone is not compatible, you will see a notice informing you of this.

Quick Concepts

1. What is the advantage of syncing your online notebook with your desktop notebook? ***p. 66***
2. What is the advantage of collaborating online with a team? ***p. 67***
3. What are the permissions options you can select when sharing a notebook and when would you use each? ***p. 67***
4. Explain the importance of versions and identifying authors of shared documents. ***p. 69***

Hands-On Exercises

2 Working Online and Collaborating with OneNote

Becky has decided to create a new OneNote notebook on OneDrive, Microsoft's online storage location free to anyone with a Microsoft account, to keep notes for her personal life. After she gets started, she realizes that some of the features she wants to use are not available in the Online App, so she will have to open the Online notebook in the desktop application.

Skills covered: Creating a OneNote Online Notebook and Opening it in OneNote 2013 • Synchronize OneNote and OneNote Online • Share a Notebook • Use Version Control and Track Multiple Authors • Install and Use Windows 8.1 OneNote App

STEP 1 » CREATING A ONENOTE ONLINE NOTEBOOK AND OPENING IT IN ONENOTE 2013

Becky has asked you to help her create a new OneNote Online notebook for personal notes. Refer to Figures 2.28 through 2.30 as you complete Step 1.

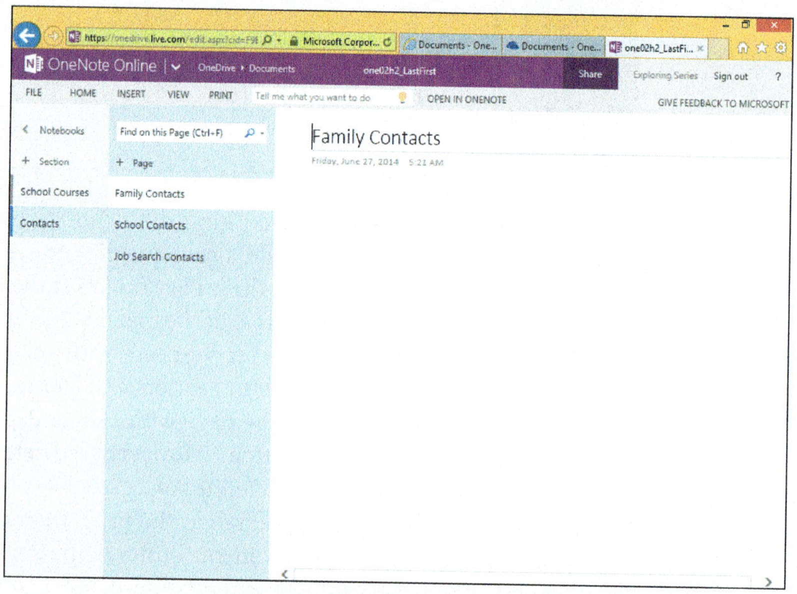

FIGURE 2.28 The notebook opened in OneNote Online App.

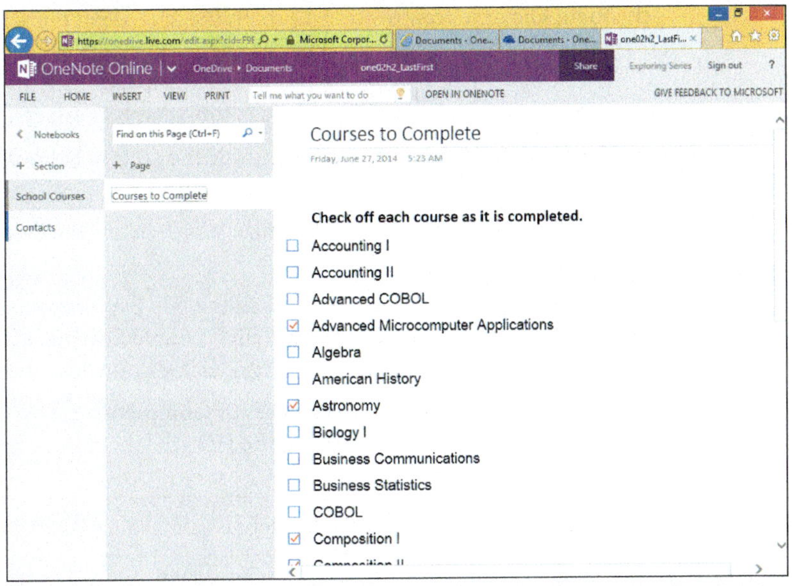

FIGURE 2.29 To Do tags have been checked off on the list.

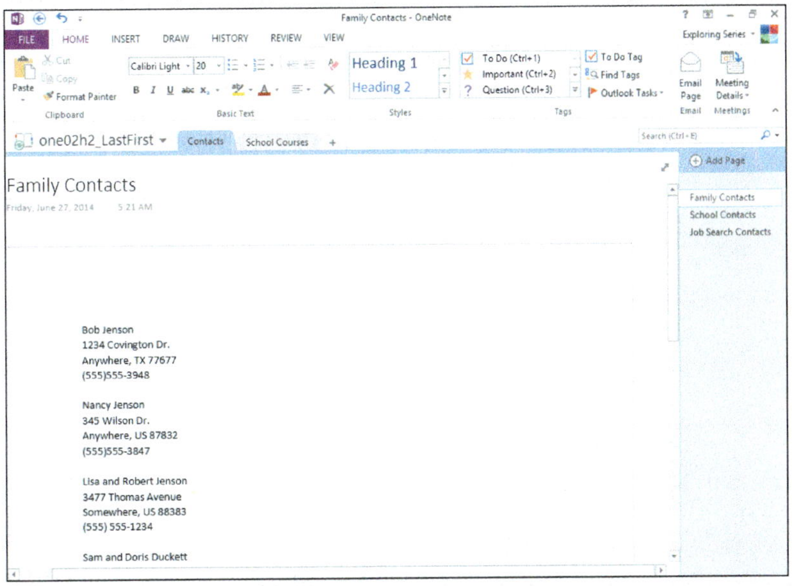

FIGURE 2.30 Content sent to the OneNote 2013 desktop application using the Send to OneNote (D) option.

TIP To Access OneDrive

To access OneDrive, you must have a Microsoft account. If you do not have a Microsoft account, you can set up a free account at:

- www.live.com
- www.outlook.com
- www.onedrive.com

a. Open Word and navigate to your student data files. Open *one02h2_OnlineApps.docx*. Type **your name** below the subtitle and then press **Enter**. Type the **current date** and then press **Enter** twice. Save the Word document as **one02h2_OnlineApps_LastFirst**.

b. Navigate to **www.onedrive.com** in **Internet Explorer**. Sign in with your Microsoft account.

c. Click **Create** on the top menu bar. Click **OneNote notebook**. In the New Microsoft OneNote notebook dialog box, type **one02h2_LastFirst** and then click **Create**.

d. Right-click the **New Section 1 tab** on the left side of the screen, in the Section pane, click **Rename**, and then type **Contacts** and then click **OK**. Enter **Family Contacts** for the page title. Click **+ Page** in the Page pane, to add a page. Title the page **School Contacts**. Add a page in the Page pane. Title the page **Job Search Contacts**.

e. Add a section in the Section pane. Title the section **School Courses**. Title the page **Courses to Complete**. Click on the **Contacts** Section tab.

f. Create a **Full-screen Snip**. Maximize Word. Below the date, paste the snip. Save and minimize Word.

g. Navigate to your student data files in the File Explorer window. Double-click *one02h2_list.docx* to open the file. If necessary, click **Enable Editing**. Press Ctrl+A to select all the text, right-click the selected text, and then click Copy. Close the Word document.

h. Click below the date in the **Courses to Complete** page on the School Courses section in OneNote Online. Click **Paste** on the HOME tab, in the Clipboard group.

> **TROUBLESHOOTING:** In the Internet Explorer security dialog box, click Allow access.

i. Click the HOME tab. At the far right of the ribbon, click the tack icon to pin the ribbon open.

j. Click to the left of Accounting 1 in the list, and then press **Enter**. Move the pointer to the blank line above Accounting 1. Type **Check off each course as it is completed**. Select the text and then right-click the selected text. Change the font to **Bold** and **16 pt**.

k. Change the font size of the listed courses to **14 pt**. Click to the left of Accounting I and then, in the Tags group of the HOME tab, click **To Do Tag**. Select the remaining course list, and then click the **To Do Tag** command to add a check box before each of the courses listed.

l. To indicate the following courses were completed, click the **check box** before:

Advanced Microcomputer Applications

Astronomy

Composition I

Composition II

Microcomputer Applications

Music Appreciation

m. Close the ribbon by clicking the up arrow (^) at the far right of the ribbon. Create a **Full-screen Snip**. Click **Edit**, and then click **Copy**. Maximize Word. Paste the snip below the previous snipped screen image.

n. Click the **Contacts** Section tab. Click below the date on the Family Contacts Page tab.

Click **OPEN IN ONENOTE** on the menu bar. Navigate to the Family Contacts page in the Contacts section in the desktop OneNote 2013 application, if necessary.

> **TROUBLESHOOTING:** If this is the first time you have opened the notebook in the OneNote desktop application, you may have to click OneNote (desktop), and then click Yes. If you have previously opened the notebook in the OneNote desktop application, you may have to click Allow to proceed, and then click Yes.

o. In Word, open *one02h2_addresses.docx* from your student data files. If necessary, click **Enable Editing**.

p. Click **Send to OneNote** in the taskbar, then click **Send to OneNote (D)**. Select the **one02h2_LastFirst** notebook in the Select Location in OneNote dialog box, expand the Contacts section, and select the **Family Contacts page**. Click **OK**.

q. Create a **Full-screen Snip** using the Snipping Tool. Maximize Word. Paste the snip below the previous snip. Save and minimize Word.

STEP 2 ›› SYNCHRONIZE ONENOTE AND ONENOTE ONLINE

Becky wants to make sure all the information she added to her notebook in the desktop OneNote application is reflected in her online OneNote notebook. She asks you to help her synchronize the two notebooks. Refer to Figure 2.31 as you complete Step 2.

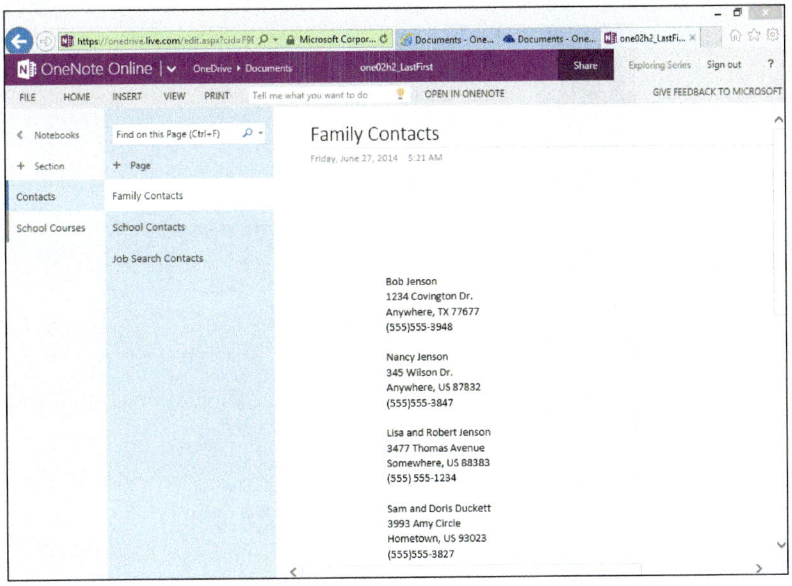

FIGURE 2.31 After syncing the notebook in the desktop application, the Family Contacts page is available in the OneNote Online App.

a. If necessary, open the *one02h2_LastFirst* notebook in the OneNote desktop application.

The notebook name is listed in the center of the screen below Notebook Information.

b. Click the **View Sync Status** button to the right of the notebook list.

c. Click **Sync Now** to the right of the one02h2_LastFirst notebook. **Close** the Shared Notebook Synchronization dialog box.

> **TROUBLESHOOTING:** If Automatic Sync is selected in the View Sync Status window, OneNote may have already synced the notebook. In this case, nothing observable will occur.

d. **Close** OneNote 2013.

e. Navigate to your OneDrive in your browser.

> **TROUBLESHOOTING:** If the OneNote Online App is not open, in the Documents folder, locate the one02h2_LastFirst OneNote file and double-click the filename to open the notebook.

f. Navigate to the Contacts section and click on the **Family Contacts** Page tab in the **one02h2_LastFirst** OneNote Online notebook.

Content added from the desktop application has been synchronized, or copied, to OneNote Online.

> **TROUBLESHOOTING:** If the Family Contacts page is blank, wait a few minutes. The addresses will appear when syncing is complete.

g. Take a **Full-screen Snip**. Maximize Word. Paste the snip below the previous snip. Save and minimize Word. Click Documents in the top menu bar. Close the one02h2_LastFirst OneNote Online notebook.

The notebook was synched to OneDrive.

STEP 3 » SHARE A NOTEBOOK

Becky's classmate, Dahlia Washington, is impressed with Becky's contacts notebook. She asked Becky to share the notebook with her. Dahlia and Becky are in the same degree program, and Dahlia is excited about the School Courses section Becky created. Because the contacts section containing personal contacts is password protected, Becky agrees. You will help Becky share her notebook. Refer to Figures 2.32 through 2.33 as you complete Step 3.

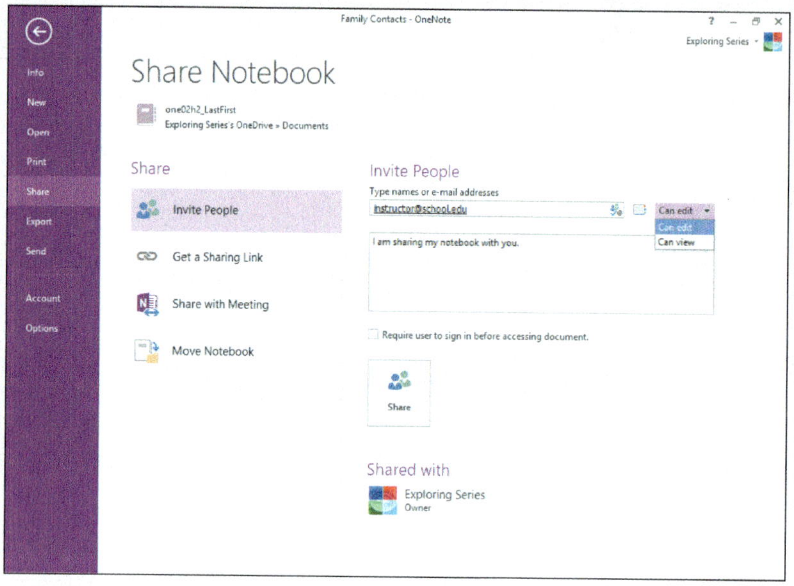

FIGURE 2.32 The Share Notebook screen enables you to invite others to share your notebook.

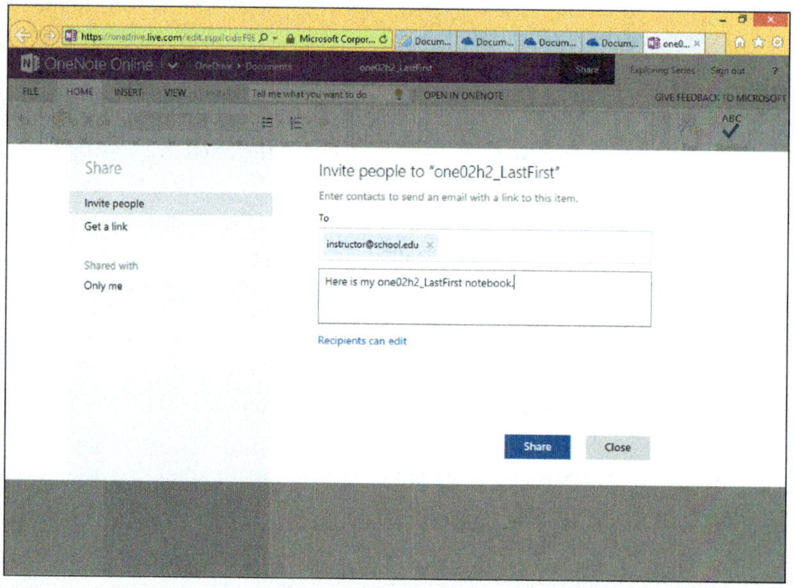

FIGURE 2.33 The OneNote Online App Share screen.

a. Open **OneNote 2013 desktop** application. Open the **one02h2_LastFirst** notebook.

b. Click the **Contacts** Section tab. Click **Password** in the Section group on the REVIEW tab. Click **Set Password**. Type **OneNote** in the Enter Password box. Type **OneNote** in the Confirm Password box. Click **OK**. Close the Password pane.

c. Use the instructions in the previous step to sync the notebook to OneDrive.

d. Click FILE. Click **Share**, and then if necessary click **Invite People**. Type **your instructor's e-mail address** in the Type names or e-mail addresses text box. Make sure **Can edit** is selected. In the personal message text box, type **I am sharing my notebook with you.**

e. Take a **Full-screen Snip** using the Snipping Tool. Maximize Word. Paste the snip below the previous snip. Save and minimize Word.

f. Do not click the **Share** button. Close OneNote 2013.

g. Open your **one02h2_LastFirst** notebook in OneDrive. Click **FILE**. Click **Share**, and then if necessary click **Share with People**. Select **Invite people** and then type **your instructor's e-mail address** in the To text box. Type **Here is my one02h2_LastFirst notebook.** in the message box.

> **TROUBLESHOOTING:** Because the Contacts section is Password Protected, a message box informing you of this may appear. If so, close the message box, and then try again. A shared notebook can have one or more password protected sections. To see protected sections, the individuals with whom you share the notebook will need to use your password.

h. Take a **Full-screen Snip** using the Snipping Tool. Maximize Word. Paste the snip below the previous snip. Save and minimize Word.

i. Click **Share**. Close one02h2_LastFirst.

STEP 4 » USE VERSION CONTROL AND TRACK MULTIPLE AUTHORS

Becky and her partner have decided to share their notebooks with each other to make it easier to share notes. Refer to Figures 2.34 and 2.35 as you complete Step 4.

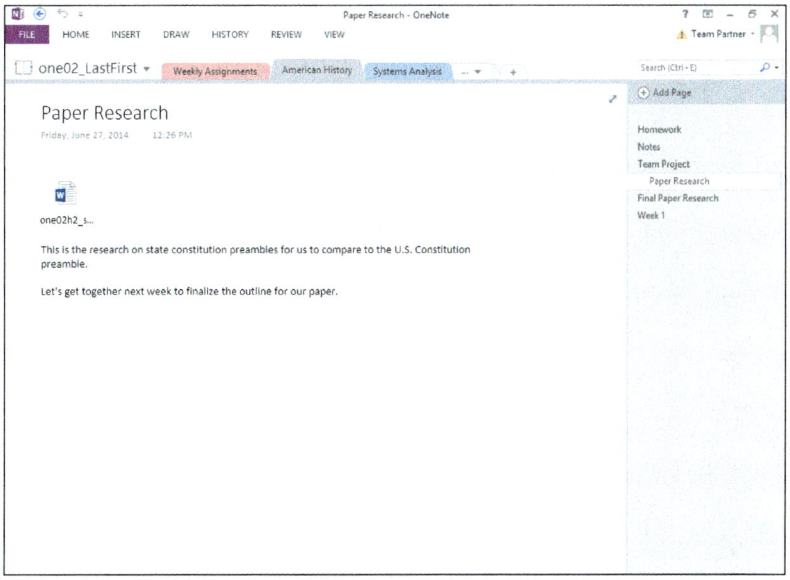

FIGURE 2.34 A file is attached to the American History Paper Research page.

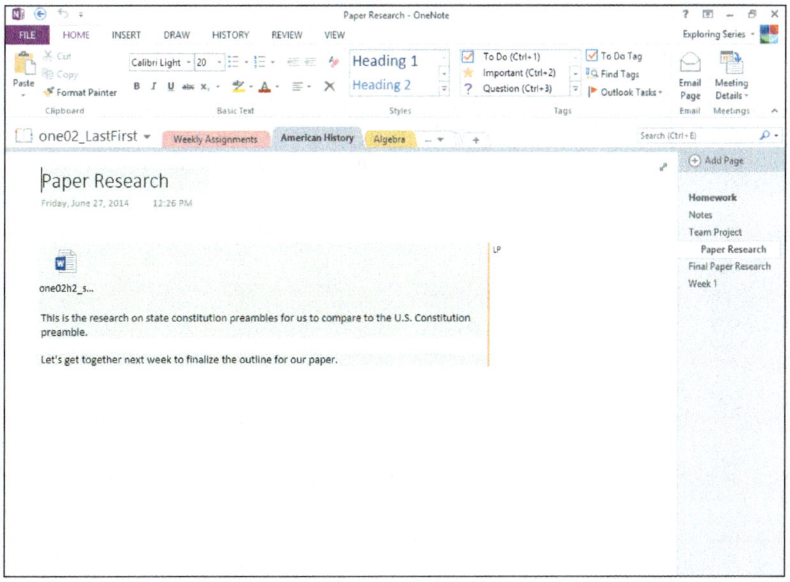

FIGURE 2.35 A vertical line with initials identifies the person who added content to a shared notebook.

TIP Partner Needed

To complete this step, you will have to have a partner. If your instructor does not assign partners, select a partner to work with for this step.

a. Open *one02_LastFirst*. **Share** your one02_LastFirst notebook with your partner using the method practiced in the previous step. Make sure your partner has editing permission. Close one02_LastFirst.

b. On OneDrive, locate **your partner's one02_PartnerName** notebook, where PartnerName is replaced by your partner's name, and **open** it. Click **EDIT NOTEBOOK**, and then click **Edit in Microsoft OneNote**. If necessary, click **Allow**, and then click **Yes**.

c. Click **OPEN IN ONENOTE**. Add a **new page** to the American History section. Move the page below the Team Project page, and right-click the Page tab. Click **Make Subpage**. Click the **Untitled** Page tab, and title the page **Paper Research**. Press Enter.

d. Click **File Attachment** in the Files group on the INSERT tab. Navigate to your student data files, and select **one02h2_state_preambles**. Click **Insert**, then select **Attach File**.

e. Type **This is the research on state constitution preambles for us to compare to the U.S. Constitution preamble.** below the attached file, Press **Enter** twice.

f. Take a **Full-screen Snip**. Maximize Word and paste the snip below the previous snip. Save and minimize Word.

g. Type **Let's get together next week to finalize the outline for our paper.**

h. Sync and close your partner's notebook.

i. Open **your own one02_LastFirst notebook** on OneDrive. Click the **VIEW** tab, and then click **Show Authors** in the Authors group.

   Notice your partner's initials on the American History section Paper Research subpage.

TROUBLESHOOTING: If your partner's initials are not showing, make sure your partner has completed the previous step, then try again.

j. Take a **Full-screen Snip**. Maximize Word. Paste the snip below the previous snip. Save and minimize Word. Close your notebook.

STEP 5 » INTRODUCTION TO WINDOWS 8.1 ONENOTE APP

Becky has just purchased a new tablet. Because the tablet has a touch screen, rather than install the full version of OneNote, she decided that she would like to install the OneNote App. Remember, the OneNote App is not the same as the OneNote Online App, which is the OneDrive version of the application. Refer to Figures 2.36 through 2.41 as you complete Step 5.

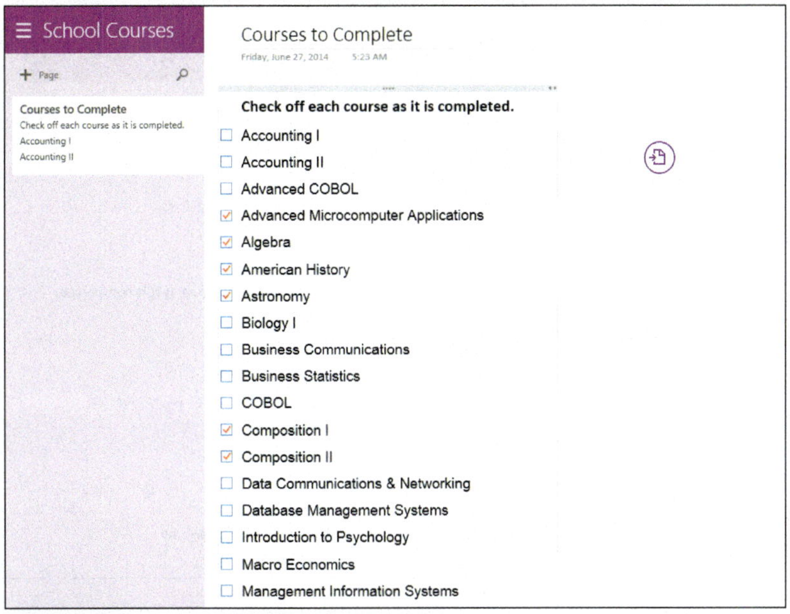

FIGURE 2.36 The School Courses Courses to Complete page open in the OneNote App.

FIGURE 2.37 Content is added to the Faculty Sponsor page in the OneNote App.

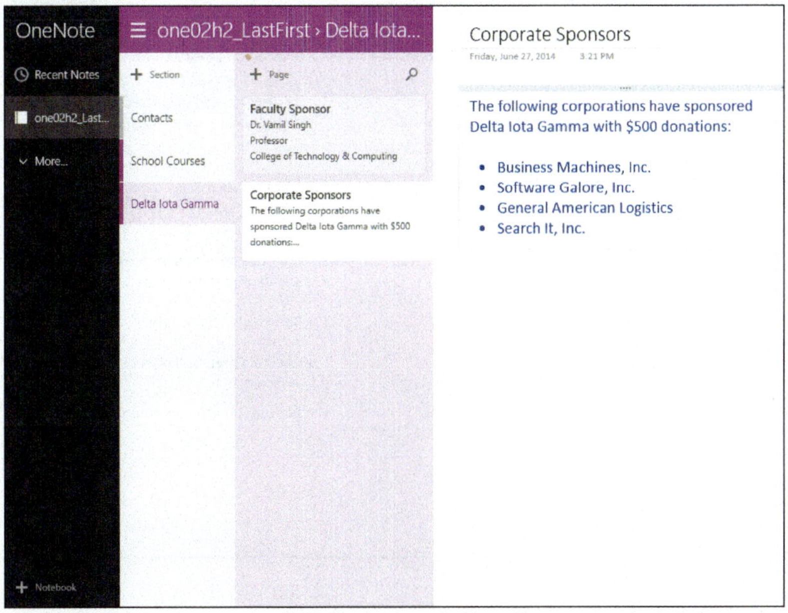

FIGURE 2.38 Text color and size can be formatted using the radial menu.

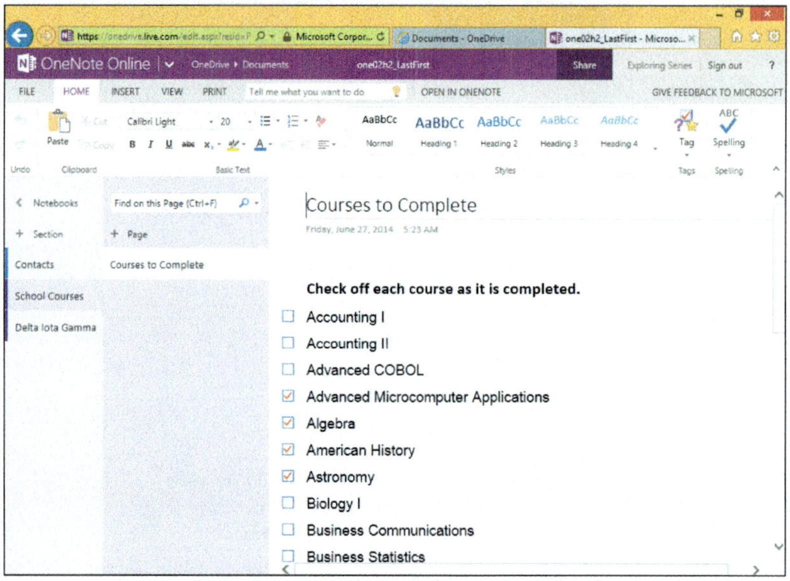

FIGURE 2.39 To Do tags checked off in the OneNote App sync to the OneNote 2013 desktop application.

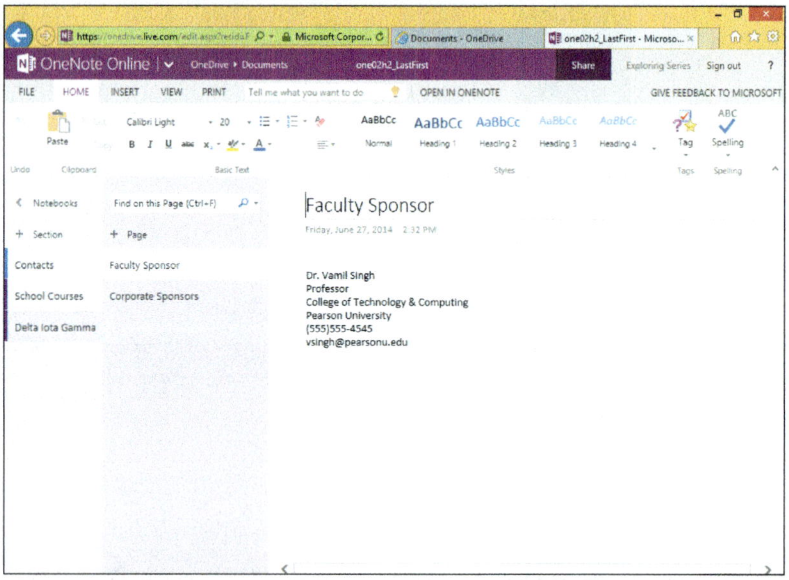

FIGURE 2.40 Faculty Sponsor information added to the OneNote App synced to the OneNote 2013 desktop application.

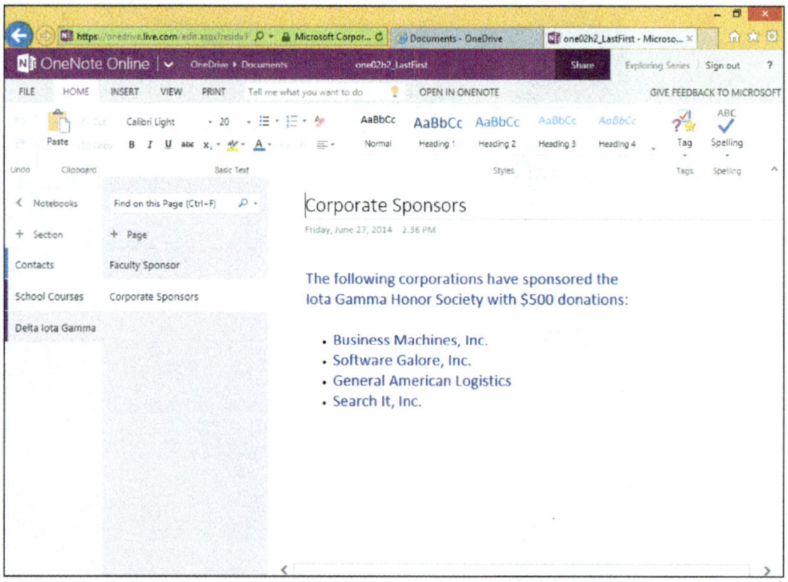

FIGURE 2.41 Formatting applied in the OneNote App synced to the OneNote 2013 desktop application.

TIP Adding an App

To complete this step, you will need to have:

- Windows 8 or Windows 8.1.
- Permission to install an app on your computer.

If you do not have Windows 8 or 8.1, you will not be able to complete the following step.

If your school does not permit you to install applications and apps on the lab computer, you will not be able to complete this step.

a. Locate and click the **Store tile** on the Windows 8.1 Start Screen.

> **TROUBLESHOOTING:** If necessary, navigate to the All Apps screen, right-click on the Store tile and at the bottom of the screen, click Pin to Start.

b. Type **OneNote** in the top right corner search box on the Store window, and then click **OneNote**. Click the **Install** button.

c. Close the Store window after the message informing you that the app has installed displays in the top right corner of the screen.

d. Locate and click the **OneNote App** tile on the Start Screen. Click **Use Express Settings** in the Welcome to OneNote window. Click **Recent Notes**.

A blank OneNote pane opens

> **TROUBLESHOOTING:** If necessary, navigate to the All Apps screen, right-click on the Store tile and at the bottom of the screen, click Pin to Start.

e. Locate and then select **one02h2_LastFirst** notebook.

> **TROUBLESHOOTING:** If an exclamation mark displays in the top right corner, you need to sign in for changes you make to sync to the online notebook. Click the exclamation mark, then click Sign In.

f. Click the **School Courses** Section tab. Click the **To Do Tag** before the following courses on the Courses to Complete page to indicate that these courses are completed:

Algebra

American History

Speech Communication

g. Click after the end of the text on the Speech Communication line and then press **Enter**. Type **Systems Analysis**. Click the **check box** before Systems Analysis to indicate that this course is completed.

h. Press the **Windows key** + **PrtScn** to take a screenshot. Maximize Word. Paste the screenshot below the previous snip. Save and minimize Word.

i. Click + **Section** to add a new section. Name the section **Delta Iota Gamma**. Click + **Page** to add a page, and name it **Faculty Sponsor**. Type the following information below the date, pressing **Enter** after each line:

   Dr. Vamil Singh

   Professor

   College of Technology & Computing

   Pearson University

   (555)555-4545

   vsingh@pearsonu.edu

j. Press the **Windows key** + **PrtScn** to take a screenshot. Maximize Word. Paste the screenshot below the previous Courses to Complete page image. Save and minimize Word.

k. Add a page titled **Corporate Sponsors**. Click below the date on the page and then type **The following corporations have sponsored Delta Iota Gamma with $500 donations:** and press **Enter** twice. Click the **radial menu button**. Click **List**. On the page, type the following, pressing **Enter** after each item:

   Business Machines, Inc.

   Software Galore, Inc.

   General American Logistics

   Search It, Inc.

   Select all the text.

   The radial menu button changes to an A.

l. Click the **A** in the center of the radial menu. Click the **arrow** at the edge of the circle by Font Size. Position and then click your mouse on **16**, and then click the **Back** button in the center of the radial menu.

m. Click the **arrow** at the edge of the Color section. Click the **arrow** next to blue. Move your pointer over the circle of colors to locate and then click on **Blue**. Click the **Back** button twice, then click outside the radial menu.

n. Press the **Windows key** + **PrtScn** to take a screenshot. Maximize Word. Paste the screenshot below the previous image. Save and minimize Word.

o. Place your **pointer** at the top edge of the screen. When the title bar displays, click the X at the far right end of the bar to close the OneNote app.

p. Open the **one02h2_LastFirst** notebook using your OneDrive OneNote Online App. Click on the Delta Iota Gamma section **Faculty Sponsor Page tab**.

q. Take a **Full-screen Snip** using the Snipping Tool. Maximize Word. Paste the snip below the previous screenshot. Save and minimize Word.

r. Click the **Delta Iota Gamma** Section tab, and then click the **Faculty Sponsor** Page tab.

s. Take a **Full-screen Snip** using the Snipping Tool. Maximize Word. Paste the snip below the previous snip. Save and minimize Word.

t. Click the **Corporate Sponsors** page tab.

u. Take a **Full-screen Snip** using the Snipping Tool. Maximize Word. Paste the snip below the previous snip. Save and close Word. Submit the Word document as directed by your instructor.

Chapter Objectives Review

After reading this chapter, you have accomplished the following objectives:

1. **Use Tools and Templates.**
    - Using Text Formatting Tools - Using the formatting commands on the HOME tab, you can change text fonts, colors, and sizes. An easy way to change formatting throughout a document is to use the Format Painter in the Clipboard group on the HOME tab.
    - Applying and Creating a Page Template - Page templates allow you to add a professionally designed page to your notebook. To find a template, click the Page Templates button, then click each major heading in the Templates pane to see what is available. Click the template you wish to use to insert a new page using that template into the document. An alternative is to create your own page template by designing the page, then saving it as a template using the Save current page as a template link at the bottom of the Templates pane.
    - Using Pen and Drawing Tools - Though primarily designed for use with tablets, touch screens, or a stylus, the pens and drawing tools available on the DRAW tab allow you to add your own art work or write text onto a page. Using a mouse with these tools is difficult, but it can be done.
    - Checking Spelling, Using a Thesaurus, and Researching a Topic - On the REVIEW tab, you can check your spelling, use a thesaurus to find the right word, or research a topic online.
    - Applying a Password - Password protection can be added to any section in a notebook. Once a section is password protected, you will need to enter the password to access the information.
    - Adding Tags - Tags help you indicate specific types information in your notebook. Tags include To Do, Critical, Question, Important, and many more. These tags appear in the notebook as symbols.
    - Searching Notes and Finding Tags - There are two ways to search for content in your notebook. First, use the Search bar to search for a word or phrase. Second, use the Find Tags command in the Tags group on the HOME page to locate information that has been tagged.
2. **Work Online and Collaborate with OneNote.**
    - Using OneNote Online App - The OneDrive OneNote Online App is available to anyone who has a Microsoft account, even if they do not own Microsoft Office 2013. Though the interface differs, the way the Online App works is very similar to that of the desktop application.
    - Creating Sections and Pages in OneNote Online App
    - Synchronizing OneNote with OneNote Online App - Using the Sync feature in OneNote allows you to have the same content notebook in all shared locations, including your desktop, OneDrive, or those with whom you have shared.
    - Sharing a Notebook - Notebooks can be shared with instructors, family members, friends, or colleagues. When you share a notebook, you determine whether those with whom the notebook is shared can only view the notebook, or if they can edit the notebook.
    - Using Version Control and Track Multiple Authors - OneNote tracks authors of changes to a shared notebook, and keeps track of versions of a notebook. This allows you to see what changes were made, as well as who made them.
3. **Install and Use Windows 8.1 OneNote App.**
    - Downloading and Installing OneNote App - The free OneNote App is available to anyone with Windows 8 or 8.1. This is the most limited version of OneNote, but it allows you to sync changes made in your notebook to OneDrive or your desktop.
    - Adding a Notebook, Section, or Page - Adding a notebook, section, or page works a little differently in OneNote App. To add a new notebook, click + Notebook at the bottom of the Notebook pane. To add a new section or page, click + Section at the top of the Section pane, or + Page at the top of the Page pane.
    - Using the Radial Menu Button - In the OneNote App, the radial menu button replaces the ribbon. When you click on a page, the radial menu appears. Click on each icon on the radial menu to open additional menus.

Key Terms Matching

For each question, locate the term that best completes the sentence. Write the letter of the correct term in the blank:

a. Password Protection
b. Template gallery
c. Find Tags
d. Toggle command
e. OneNote App
f. OneNote Online App
g. Format Painter
h. Page template
i. Pass phrase
j. Search term
k. Share
l. OneDrive
m. Sync
n. Tag
o. Online app

1. The ________ command makes it easy to find marked content in a notebook. **p. 53**
2. ________ is Microsoft's note taking software designed primarily for touch screen tablets and smartphones. **p. 70**
3. A(n) ________ is an electronic marker inserted into a page to mark specific types of content. **p. 52**
4. A(n) ________ is a command that is either on or off. **p. 52**
5. A(n) ________ is a pre-designed format used for OneNote pages. **p. 48**
6. A(n) ________ is a key word or group of words used to narrow down returned results. **p. 53**
7. ________ is used to make a notebook the same on all platforms. **p. 66**
8. The ________ command allows you to provide access to your OneNote notebooks to others. **p. 67**
9. A(n) ________ is a group of words used as a password, or as the base for a password made up of the initials of the words. **p. 53**
10. The ________ allows users to copy the formatting of one selection and paste it to another section. **p. 48**
11. A(n) ________ contains a selection of pre-designed and formatted pages that can be inserted into a section. **p. 49**
12. ________ is the version of the note taking software used in OneDrive. **p. 63**
13. A(n) ________ is a limited function application available for use through OneDrive. **p. 63**
14. ________ is an online storage platform that also provides access to limited versions of some web-based Microsoft Office applications. **p. 63**
15. ________ prevents unauthorized individuals seeing or adding content to a section. **p. 51**

Multiple Choice

1. To copy the format of a section of text to another section, use the:
   (a) Copy and Paste buttons
   (b) Format Copy
   (c) Format Painter
   (d) Format Dialog Box

2. The commands on the ________ tab allow you to check versions and review who made changes to a shared notebook.
   (a) VIEW
   (b) HISTORY
   (c) HOME
   (d) REVIEW

3. Which sharing option would be used to allow multiple people to access a notebook?
   (a) Invite People
   (b) Get a Sharing Link
   (c) Share with Meeting
   (d) Move Notebook

4. Which of the following is the best password?
   (a) abcd1234
   (b) redfern
   (c) PWwiue35;k
   (d) 1234546abc

5. To protect information in a section in your notebook, you can:
   (a) Add password protection
   (b) Delete the section
   (c) Hide the section
   (d) Move the section to OneDrive

6. Which of the following mistakes will the Spelling checker **NOT** find?
   (a) I senpt two nihts in London, England.
   (b) Win I have enough money, I am taking a trip to France.
   (c) The tour was overbookd and I had to wait in the bus station for three hours.
   (d) The train was late getting to the stashun.

7. Which of the following is **NOT** an Online App available in OneDrive?
   (a) OneNote Online App
   (b) Access Online App
   (c) Word Online App
   (d) PowerPoint App

8. An easy way to add pre-designed page designs and formats to a OneNote notebook is to use a:
   (a) Page form
   (b) Section template
   (c) Section form
   (d) Page template

9. To Do, Contact, Book to Read, Important, and Idea are examples of:
   (a) Tips
   (b) Tags
   (c) Notations
   (d) Bookmarks

10. Which of the following is available for free through the Windows store?
    (a) OneDrive
    (b) OneNote App
    (c) OneNote Online App
    (d) OneNote 2013

Practice Exercises

1 Update an Existing Notebook

Janetta has decided to team up with two other sewing enthusiasts on her blog. She will be working with Becky and her neighbor, Megan. Whereas she likes the notebook you created for her, she asked you to make some formatting changes.

> **NOTES:** This practice exercise is based on the Chapter 1 Practice 2 exercise solution. After completing this exercise, you will submit the notebook by sharing it with your instructor.

a. Open **the one01_p2_LastFirst** notebook created in Chapter 1 Practice 2. Click **File**, click **Export**, click **Notebook**, and then if necessary click **OneNote Package (*.onepkg)**. Click **Export**. Navigate to your storage device, name the file **one02_p1_LastFirst**. Make sure the file type is **OneNote Single File Package**, and then click **Save**.

b. If necessary, in the Unpack Notebook dialog box, **browse** to your storage device, and then click **Create**. Close the one01_p2_LastFirst notebook, and open **one02_p1_LastFirst** notebook.

> **TROUBLESHOOTING:** The prompt to unpack the notebook usually happens the first time you open an exported notebook. If you do not get this prompt, skip step b.

c. In the Affiliate Programs section, click the **Applied Programs** Page tab. Select the **top table row contents**. Click **Bold** in the Basic Text group on the HOME tab. Change the font size to **12 pt**.

d. Right-click the cell containing *Date Applied*, click **Table**, and then click **Insert Right**. Type **Commission**. Press **Tab** four times. Type **4%** and then press **Tab** four times. Type **18%** and then press **Tab** four times. Type **10%**. If necessary, with your pointer on the right edge of the text container, drag the side to the right until all first row text is on one line.

e. Add a section and name it **Research**. On the INSERT tab, in the Pages group, add a **Glasses Corner** template from the Decorative category. Title the page **Article Topic:** (include the colon) and then press **Enter**.

f. Type **Resources:** (include the colon) and then press **Enter** three times.

g. Type **Images:** (include the colon) and then press Enter four times.

h. Type **Notes:** (include the colon).

i. Delete the Untitled page. If the Templates pane is not open, then click the top half of the **Page Templates** button in the Pages group on the INSERT tab. Click **Save current page as a template**. Type **Articles** in the Template name text box, and then click **Save**. **Close** the Templates pane.

j. Change the title to **Article Topic: Reading Sewing Patterns**. Open your browser and navigate to **Google.com**. Search for **reading sewing patterns**. Locate and click **Reading a Sewing Pattern—For Dummies**. **Copy** the URL in the address box.

k. In OneNote, on the Article Topic: Reading Sewing Patterns page, click at the end of Resources: and then press **Enter** twice.

l. Press **CTRL+V** to paste the URL. Click **Numbering** in the Basic Text group on the HOME tab, and then press **Enter**.

m. Using the same technique, locate two other online articles about reading sewing patterns, and paste the URLs, pressing Enter after the second article added to the list.

   You will now have a list of three online resources.

n. Click below **Images:** on the page. Click the **INSERT** tab. Click **Online Pictures** in the Images group. Search Office.com Clip Art for **sewing pattern**. Select the **second image** (pattern pieces on a blue background) and then click **Insert**.

o. Click at the end of Notes: and press **Enter** twice. Click **Research** in the Spelling group on the REVIEW tab. In the Search for: text box, type **reading a sewing pattern**. Scroll through the results returned in the Research pane to locate **Read a Pattern—Learning Sewing**. Click the **URL** below the listing (http://www.burdastyle.com/techniques/read-a-pattern). If this listing does not display, use your browser to navigate to the URL. Scroll in your browser until the paragraph beginning "Just starting to use patterns?" completely displays at the bottom of the screen. Click Send to OneNote, click **Send to OneNote Screen Clipping (S)**. Click and drag to select the image through the end of the paragraph beginning "Just starting to use patterns?"

p. Expand the **one02_p1_LastFirst** notebook. Expand the **Research** Section tab. Click the **Article Topic: Reading Sewing Patterns**, and then click **Send to Selected Location**. **Close** the Research pane.

q. Click the **Blog** Section tab, and then click the **Sewing Tips** page. Below the image, click before Centimeter. Insert an **Important tag** from the Tags group on the HOME tab.

r. Sync the notebook. Export the notebook and submit it according to directions.

2 Password Protect a Section, Edit the Notebook in OneNote App

Janetta has decided that the Earnings section should not be available to her team. She has asked you to help her password protect the Earnings section.

NOTES: This practice exercise is based on the Chapter 1 Practice 2 exercise solution. After completing this exercise, you will submit the notebook by sharing it with your instructor.

a. Open the **one02_p1_LastFirst** notebook created in Practice 1. Click **File**, click **Export**, click **Notebook**, and then if necessary click **OneNote Package (*.onepkg)**. Click **Export**. Navigate to your storage device, name the file **one02_p2_LastFirst**. Make sure the file type is **OneNote Single File Package**, and then click **Save**.

b. Close **one02_p1_LastFirst**. In the File Explorer window, navigate to the file exported as one02_p2_LastFirst and double-click the file name. In the Unpack Notebook dialog box, click **Create**.

c. Click the **Earnings** Section tab. Click **Password** in the Section group on the REVIEW tab. Click **Set Password** in the Password Protection pane. In the Enter Password text box, type **OneNote**. Type **OneNote** in the Confirm Password text box, and then click **OK**. **Close** the Password Protection pane.

d. Click **FILE**, click **Share**. If necessary, select your **OneDrive account**. **Sign in** using your e-mail and password. Type **one02_p2_LastFirst** in the Notebook Name box, and then click **Move Notebook**. Click **OK**. If necessary, select your **OneDrive**, and then click **Invite People**. In the Type names or e-mail addresses, type **your instructor's e-mail**. Make sure *Can edit* is selected. In the message box, type **My notebook is one02_p2_LastFirst**.

e. Using the Snipping Tool, take a **Full-screen Snip**. Save the snip as **one02_p2_share_LastFirst**. Close the Snipping Tool, and then click **Share**.

f. In your Windows 8.1 Start Screen, click the **OneNote App tile**. In the OneNote App, open **one02_p2_LastFirst**. Click the **Schedule** Section tab. At the bottom of the screen, click **Delete Section**, and then click **Delete Section**. The Earnings Section will display a message: Sorry, we can't open this section because it is protected.

g. Click the Blog section **Ideas for Articles** Page tab. Click in the page, and then click the **radial menu button**. Click the **List arrow**. Click the **arrow bullet point**. Type **Choosing the right needle** and then press **Enter**. Type **Sewing for children** and then press **Enter**. Type **Selecting the right fabric**.

h. Close the OneNote App. Open your **one02_p2_LastFirst** in OneDrive Online App. Notice the bullet points on the Ideas for Articles page. Close the notebook.

i. Open your OneNote 2013 on your desktop and open **one02_p2_LastFirst**. Click **FILE**, click **Info** on the left side of the screen, click **View Sync Status**, and then click the **Sync Now** button to the right side of the notebook name. Notice the bullet points on the Ideas for Articles page.

j. Export as **one02_p2_LastFirst** the notebook and submit it according to your instructor's directions. Close OneNote 2013.

Mid-Level Exercises

1 Create a Notebook for the Iota Gamma Honor Society

Dr. Vamil Singh, the campus faculty sponsor of the Iota Gamma Honor Society, has asked you to create a OneNote notebook that will enable her to keep Honor Society members updated on current events and activities. Dr. Singh would like to provide View Only access to all members of the society so that they can see flyers on upcoming events, read meeting minutes, and learn about available scholarships. However, she needs the Scholarship Applicants page to be password protected.

This exercise will be submitted by sharing the notebook with your instructor.

a. Sign into OneDrive. Create a notebook using the OneNote Online App. Name the notebook **one02_m1_LastFirst**. If necessary, click **Enable Editing**. Name the Untitled Section **Delta Iota Gamma**. In the Delta Iota Gamma section, name the untitled page **Members**. Add a section titled **Scholarship**. In the Scholarship section, add two pages titled **Scholarships**, and **Scholarship Applicants**.

b. Share the notebook with your instructor. Open the notebook in the OneNote desktop application.

c. On the Members page, insert the **one02_m1_small_logo** data file image and then press **Enter**. Insert a **File Printout** of the **one02_m1_members** data file.

d. Add a **Glasses Corner** page template to the Delta Iota Gamma section. Title the page **Meeting Agenda**. Insert a **File Printout** of the **one02_m1_agenda** student data file to the Meeting Agenda page.

e. Add a page and title it **Meeting Minutes**. On the Meeting Minutes page, insert a **File Printout** of the **one02_m1_minutes** student data file. Make the Meeting Agenda page a **subpage** to the Meeting Minutes.

f. On the Scholarships page, use **File Printout** to print out the **one02_m1_scholarship** student data file.

g. On the Scholarship Applicants page, type **Students Applying for the Wilson B. Graham Honor Society Scholarship** and then press **Enter**. Change the text to **Arial Black**, change the font size to **11.5 pt**, and change the font color **Green, Darker 25%**.

h. Click below *Students Applying for the Wilson B. Graham Honor Society Scholarship*, and then type the following information, pressing **Tab** after each item in the first column, and pressing **Enter** after each row except the last row:

Student	**GPA**
Susie Pace	**3.90**
Antonio Ruiz	**3.89**
Melody Luz	**3.90**
Ahn Min Joon	**4.0**
Tom Ayers	**4.0**
Bob Franklin	**3.86**

i. In your OneNote 2013 desktop application, **Export** your notebook to your storage device, and name it **one02_m1_LastFirst**.

2 Edit a Shared Notebook, Edit a Notebook in OneNote App

TIP Partner Needed

The following steps will require you to work with a partner. If you do not have a partner, check with your instructor.

a. Open **one02_m1_Last First**. **Export** your one02_m1_LastFirst notebook to your storage device, and name it **one02_m2_LastFirst** Unpack the notebook, and then Share your notebook with your partner and your instructor. Close OneNote.

b. Open Outlook. When you receive the invitation to share your partner's notebook, open the e-mail and click the **name of your partner's notebook**. If necessary, click **Continue**. Close, Outlook.

c. Sign into your **OneDrive** account. Locate your partner's **one02_m2_PartnerName** notebook on OneDrive, where PartnerName is replaced by your partner's LastFirst name, and open it. Click **Edit in Microsoft OneNote**. If necessary, click **Allow**, and then click **Yes.**

The notebook opens in the Microsoft OneNote 2013 desktop application.

d. On the **Members** page, click below the list of members. Type **New Members for Spring 2017** and then press **Enter** twice.

e. Type the following, pressing **Enter** after each name:

YourName

Bradley Simmons

f. Sync the notebook to OneDrive and then close the notebook.

g. From your Windows 8 Start Screen, open your **one02_m2_LastFirst** notebook in **OneNote App**. Add a section titled **Prospects** and then title the untitled page **Prospective Members.**

h. Below the page headings, type **The following individuals have been sent invitations to join Delta Iota Gamma**. Press **Enter** twice.

i. Type the following names, pressing **Enter** after each:

Nancy Cordova

John Shackling

Jennifer Bell

Alexander Grant

j. Select *The following individuals have been sent invitations to join Delta Iota Gamma*. Use the radial menu to change the font to **13 pt**. Change the font color to **Dark Blue** and **Bold** the text.

k. Close the OneNote App. Open your **one02_m2_LastFirst** notebook in the OneNote 2013 desktop application. For all sections, check spelling, correcting errors as necessary.

l. Password protect the Scholarship section using **OneNote** as the password.

m. Close the Password pane.

n. On the **Prospective Members** page, add a **Schedule meeting tag** from the Tags Gallery before each of the four names listed.

o. Because the Honor Society will be sending three students and Dr. Singh to the national convention in New Orleans, you need to locate three Web sites where airline tickets can be purchased. Create a new section titled **Travel Plans**. Title the untitled page **Tickets**. Using the **Research** tool on the **REVIEW** tab, locate **three Web sites that offer airline tickets**. Copy each of the three URLs and paste them in the **Tickets** page, pressing **Enter** after pasting each. Close the Research pane.

p. **Export** the complete notebook to your storage media. Close OneNote 2013. If the OneDrive OneNote Online App is open, close the notebook, and log out of OneDrive. Submit the exported notebook as directed by your instructor.

Beyond the Classroom

General Case

Create a presentation for incoming freshmen on how using OneNote helps you keep up with course work and helps in preparation for exams. The presentation requirements are:

- Name the presentation **one02_gc_OneNote_LastFirst.**
- A cover slide with an appropriate title and all team member's names in the subtitle.
- An introductory slide that explains what the presentation will cover.
- A minimum of six slides of content.
- At least two appropriate images of your choice (these can be screenshots).
- A summary slide.
- A works cited slide with all images, including screenshots.

Submit the presentation as directed by your instructor.

Research Case

Microsoft OneNote works with a variety of apps for your phone, tablet, or laptop. Visit **http://www.onenote.com/apps**. Review the apps Microsoft recommends. Write a one- or two-page paper answering the following questions

- Which apps would you be interested in using? Explain why.
- What other apps do you think might be useful to use with OneNote?

Save your document as **one02_rc_Apps_LastFirst**. Make sure your name and the current date are on the first two lines at the top of the first page. Submit the document as directed by your instructor.

Soft Skills Case

Dr. Singh is so impressed with your OneNote skills, she has asked you to create a basic OneNote Notebook for her Instructional Design students to use. Name the notebook **ID Class Notebook** The notebook should include the following Section tabs:

Syllabus
Class Notes
Homework
Research
Instructor Documents

Use at least two page templates in creating in the notebook. Delete all unnamed sections and pages before submitting the notebook.

Export the notebook as a .onepkg file named **one02_ss_IDClassNotebook_LastFirst.**

Submit the exported notebook as directed by your instructor.

Capstone Exercise

Programming Team Notebook

As a student intern for Search It, Inc., you have been asked to add content to an existing OneNote notebook for the Server Side Programming Team. The notebook contains sections and pages to provide information and announcements to the team.

For this assignment, you will need to work with a partner. This assignment will be submitted by sharing the notebook with your instructor.

a. Open **one01_capstone_LastFirst** in OneNote 2013 desktop application. Export the notebook to your storage device as a OneNote Package (*.onepkg) named **one02_capstone_LastFirst**

b. Close one01_capstone_LastFirst. Open **one02_capstone_LastFirst.**

c. Add a section named **Manager**. Add a **Binoculars Corner** template page. Name the template page **Management Training**. Save the page as a template named **Management**. Close the Templates pane.

d. Delete the untitled page. Insert a **file printout** of the **one02_c_flyer** data file on the Management Training page. Because the entire team will have access to the notebook, the Manager section needs to be password protected. **Password protect** the Manager section using **OneNote** as the password. Close the Password Protection pane.

e. Share the notebook with your partner and your instructor. Sync and close the notebook. Navigate to OneDrive. Open your partner's **one02_capstone_PartnerName** notebook, where PartnerName is replaced by your partner's LastFirst name. Click **Edit in OneNote.**

f. In the **Activities** section, add a page and name it **Team Activities**. Type **Print the attached file, fill in your preferences, and give the completed survey to the team administrative assistant by Tuesday.** Press **Enter** twice. Attach the **one02_c_survey** data file.

g. Sync and close your partner's notebook.

h. Open your **one02_capstone_LastFirst** notebook with your desktop OneNote 2013 application. On the Team Activities page, below the previous content, insert the **one01_c_results** spreadsheet as an **Existing Excel Spreadsheet**. Click below the inserted spreadsheet, press **Enter**, and then type **We will have a potluck at our manager's house for our monthly team outing.** Press **Enter.**

i. On the **Activities section Company Activities** page, highlight the **page title**. Change the font to **Brush Script**. Change the font size to **36 pt**. Change the font color to **Blue, Darker 50%.**

j. Highlight the **page title**. Use the **Format Painter** to format all page titles in all sections the same as the **Activities Company Activities** page except the Manager section.

k. Sync and close one02_capstone_LastFirst.

l. If necessary, log into OneDrive. On your Windows 8 Start Screen, open the **OneNote Online App**. Navigate to the **Team Shirts** subpage. Bold the header text in the first row of the table.

m. Add a page to the **Notes section** and title it **JavaScript** and press **Enter**. Select the JavaScript page title, change the font to **Brush Script MT**. Change the font size to **36 pt**. Change the font color to **Dark Blue.**

n. Type **Use these reference sites for JavaScript coding questions:** and then press **Enter** twice. Using a **diamond-shaped bullet list**, type the following, pressing **Enter** after the first two URLs:

   www.w3schools.com/js/default.asp

   www.javascriptsource.com/tutorials

   www.landofcode.com/javascript-tutorials/

o. Close OneNote App. In your desktop OneNote 2013 application, **Sync** the notebook. View the JavaScript page in your notebook.

p. Export one02_capstone_LastFirst to your storage device. If instructed to do so, submit the exported notebook to your instructor. Close OneNote 2013. Close OneDrive.

Glossary

Container An area on a page that is used to hold text, images, or other content.

Export The method of backing up or saving the notebook to a different storage location.

Find Tags A command on the HOME tab that makes it possible to locate specific tags in your notebook.

Format Painter A tool that allows the format of selected text or an object to be copied and pasted to another text selection or object.

Merge The technique used to combine the contents of two or more pages, sections, or notebooks.

Notebook A file created by OneNote to hold content divided into sections and pages.

Notebook pane Lists open notebooks to allow easy switching between notebooks.

OneDrive A free online storage platform that also provides users with access to limited versions of some web-based Microsoft Office applications.

OneNote 2013 Microsoft's most recent version of OneNote, which is note-taking software designed specifically for the desktop computer.

OneNote App The version of OneNote created primarily for touch screen tablets and smartphones.

OneNote Online App Microsoft's OneDrive version of the OneNote application.

Online App A limited function application that is available on the OneDrive platform.

Optical Character Recognition (OCR) The capability to convert an image into text.

Page Content area inside OneNote sections.

Page pane The area on the OneNote screen that displays tabs for all pages located within the selected section.

Page template A pre-designed format used for OneNote pages.

Pass phrase A phrase used as a password or used as a reminder of a password by using the initials of all words in the phrase for a password.

Password protection A means of preventing unauthorized individuals from seeing or editing protected sections.

Path The exact route a computer uses to locate a file.

Quick note A note that has not been placed into a specific page.

Quick Access Toolbar A mini toolbar that contains four command buttons: Back, Undo, Dock to Desktop, and Customize.

Ribbon The area across the top of the OneNote screen that contains tabs with commands used for formatting and managing content in the pages.

Screenshot An image created from the content displayed on your monitor.

Search bar A tool that allows users to locate specific information or specific types of information in a notebook, section, or page.

Search scope Settings that determine where OneNote looks when searching for information users need to find.

Search term A phrase or key word used in a search to narrow the returned results of a search.

Section The primary division in a notebook, each of which may contain one page or many pages.

Section tab The tabs that provide easy access to sections in the notebook.

Share A feature that allows users to give access to their notebooks to other individuals.

Subpage A page indented below a previous page.

Snipping Tool A tool included in Windows Vista, Windows 7, and Windows 8 accessory applications that is designed to capture screenshots.

Sync Saves an exact duplicate of changes made in OneNote 2013, OneNote Online App, and OneNote App, so that all versions of the application have access to the same information.

Tag An electronic marker inserted into a page to mark specific types of content.

Template gallery The location of page templates, including user designed page templates.

Toggle command Any command that is either on or off. Clicking once turns it on, while clicking a second time turns it off.

Index